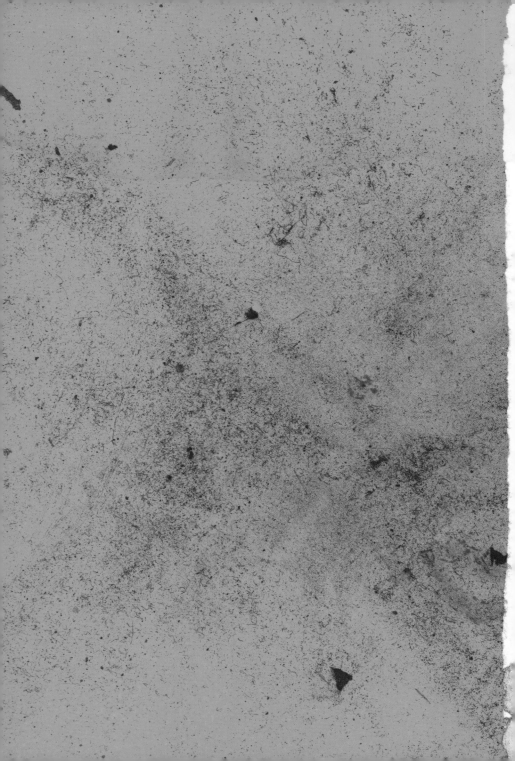

LOST

A HISTORY OF DISAPPEARANCES

LOST

A HISTORY OF DISAPPEARANCES

THE WORLD'S MOST PERPLEXING COLD CASES & UNSOLVED MYSTERIES

FROM AMELIA EARHART TO THE BERMUDA TRIANGLE,
D. B. COOPER & THE LOST COLONY OF ROANOKE

ILLUSTRATIONS BY NEIL EVANS

CIDER MILL
PRESS

BOOK
PUBLISHERS

CONTENTS

CHAPTER 2: INTO THIN AIR

CHAPTER 3: INTO THE WILD

CHAPTER 4: INTO THE DEPTHS

CHAPTER 5: DRIVING INTO THE ABYSS

CHAPTER 6: YOUTH STOLEN: CHILDREN, TEENAGERS, AND STUDENTS

CHAPTER 7: MODERN-DAY MYSTERIES

INTRODUCTION

We've all heard about the most notorious cases of missing persons, missing families, or even whole towns seemingly vanishing. Whether it was trying to solve the mysteries of the Roanoke Colony or Amelia Earhart when we first learned about them in elementary school, or following the latest stories on the news, these mysteries have been a universal source of fascination for ages. Maybe you're the kind of person who studies these cases religiously and has vowed never to travel to the Bermuda Triangle lest you fall victim to whatever sinister forces may inhabit it, or maybe you're someone who wants to know more about the stories behind these famous—or infamous—names.

This book will give you the inside scoop on the most intriguing instances of people seemingly vanishing. First, take a trip to the past and peruse some of the mysteries that have gone unsolved for dozens or even hundreds of years. The Grand Duchess Anastasia Nikolaevna of Russia, the Lindbergh Baby, and the Sodder Children are just a few of history's greatest disappearances. Then, learn all about people who vanished in midair, into the wilderness, and into the murky depths of the sea. The tales of Malaysia Airlines Flight 370, Vermont's infamous Long Trail, and the *Mary Celeste* are joined by plenty more that you won't soon forget (particularly when you're planning your next vacation). Even traveling close to home can be dangerous, as we'll learn in the chapter filled with stories of those who drove into the night, never to be seen again. *Lost* concludes with modern-day mysteries: mysteries involving children, teens, and students, like Madeleine McCann and Natalee Holloway, and adults, like Sukumara Kurup and the Springfield Three.

We've summed up the most essential facts of each story, but in most cases no one really knows how they ended. Try to work out for yourself what may have happened to these people, many of whom appear to have walked off the face of the earth. Use the fundamental information you find here, or let it inspire you to do deeper research on the mysteries that most capture your attention. You never know what one more set of fresh eyes on a case might uncover. Or perhaps you're the kind of person who doesn't need to strive toward a conclusion in order to enjoy a good story. You may just want to leave the endings to your imagination. There is certainly a wide range of possibilities as far as answers go, and we may never know for sure.

What we do know is that over 600,000 people go missing in the United States alone each year. These stories are a drop in the bucket of a troubling, bewildering, and riveting issue. Whether you want to untangle these mysteries, simply ponder the evidence, or avoid becoming a lost soul yourself, this book is only the beginning.

CHAPTER 1
HISTORY'S GREATEST DISAPPEARANCES

IT'S A TALE AS OLD AS TIME. In the earliest days of humanity, the consequences of getting lost were deadly. Many things have changed over the years, but this principle seems to have remained constant. It's hard to say for sure, however, as the nature of the event is inherently mysterious. While death affords a kind of certainty, disappearance leaves questions. The kind of questions that people spend decades, even centuries, trying to answer. This chapter will take you through some of the mysteries that people have been trying to solve for many years, all occurring before 1950 and going as far back as 1302.

THE LOST COLONY
OF ROANOKE

One of the great mysteries of English history, the fate of the Roanoke Colony, continues to mystify and baffle even after more than 400 years. Roanoke was an English colony founded on an island off the coast of modern North Carolina. About 100 men and women settled there, planning to make it a permanent home and sell crops they produced, including sassafras, which was valued as a medicine.

The governor of the colony was John White, and he and a small number of people sailed back to England in 1587 to get extra supplies before winter, so that the people back at Roanoke could be more comfortable and better face the challenges of cold weather and a strange land. But at that time, England and Spain were approaching war with each other. By 1588, Spain launched a fleet of ships called the Armada to try to take England by force and remove Queen Elizabeth I from the throne. The English (with the help of some very bad weather) defeated the Spanish, but that didn't settle the matter, and it was dangerous to be on the open oceans. White wasn't able to get back to Roanoke until 1590, and when he did, he was in for quite a surprise.

The entire colony was deserted. And there was no information about what had happened to them—except for one small clue. White found a word carved on a wooden post that said "Croatoan," which was the name of another island close by, as well as of the Native Americans who lived in the area. But what did this mean? Did the Roanoke colonists have to leave, and did they relocate to Croatoan?

Some thought this was the case at the time, but there wasn't any evidence of them being there either.

So what happened to them? Some believe friendly Native Americans may have taken in the colonists, who, over time, became full members of their society, moving farther inland and giving up their colony. But this seems unlikely, as there were such large differences between the two cultures.

Others think that a group of Native Americans hostile to the colonists may have attacked, but there was no evidence of a fight, no bodies, and no signs of violence.

Another group believes the colonists tried to return to England, and either sank at sea or were attacked by a Spanish ship, because England and Spain were still at war. But their ship wouldn't have fit all of them on board.

Maybe it was some kind of combination of these events? Were the colonists attacked, and did some seek refuge with a group of friendly Native Americans, while others tried to sail back to England to warn Elizabeth's government, when they were attacked or sank? It's possible, but it is odd that no record of what happened was left behind. Or maybe there was, and someone else took it? Again, the Roanoke story remains one of the biggest mysteries of English/early American history.

BENJAMIN BATHURST

Benjamin Bathurst was a young diplomat working for the British government. In 1809, he was sent to Vienna to try to persuade the government of Austria to join an alliance against Napoleon, who, to put it lightly, was causing all kinds of problems in Europe at the time. Being a diplomat in those circumstances was a difficult and dangerous job, and Bathurst no doubt had enemies and spies watching what he was doing. He was returning to England through Germany in November of that year, pretending to be a merchant and using a false name to hide his identity.

On November 25, he stopped at an inn in the town of Perleberg, west of Berlin. People who saw him there said he seemed nervous and waited for several hours in a small room at the inn. The coach had been delayed, and new horses weren't ready to pull it until about 9:00 p.m. When Bathurst was finally told that the coach was ready, he left the room at once and headed straight for it...and never made it. Herr Krause, the driver of the coach, returned to it a few minutes later and was surprised to see that Bathurst was not there. A quick search revealed that he was nowhere to be found. In fact, he was never seen again. No one at the inn saw him come back, and soldiers guarding the street said they hadn't seen anyone come their way. Later on, Napoleon insisted his agents had nothing to do with the disappearance, and offered his assistance to Bathurst's wife in clearing up the mystery. A search of the area revealed some of his clothing, but nothing else.

So, what happened to poor Benjamin? No one really knows. He might have been the victim of a mugging or murder, but a body was never found.

In 1852, a skeleton was found buried under a stable. There were signs that the back of the head had been hit by an object. It might have been Benjamin, but in the days before forensic science, no one could say for sure. And it still doesn't answer the question of how he could have been attacked and even killed in complete silence, and how the killers dragged him away without being seen or heard. It was as if he had walked toward the coach and just vanished.

DOROTHY HARRIET CAMILLE ARNOLD

On December 12, 1910, Dorothy Arnold did something amazing—she vanished, but not in the way so typical of these kinds of stories. She didn't go out into the remote woods, or walk into a cave, or get in a car and go for a drive. She vanished in the middle of New York, one of the busiest cities in the world, in the middle of the afternoon.

Arnold came from a very wealthy family and never had to worry about money. Instead, because she had a college degree in literature, she wanted to be a writer. Her parents didn't really approve; it was the early 20th century, and what they wanted was for her to be married. But Arnold was

determined. In the spring of 1910, she submitted a story to a magazine called *McClure's*, but it was rejected.

Instead of being supportive of her, her friends and family teased her, which was a terrible thing to do!

Still, she was determined. She submitted another story to the same magazine in the fall of 1910, which was also rejected. She was really upset about this but, again, got no support or comfort from her friends and family.

On December 12, Arnold went out to buy a new gown for her sister's upcoming party. She also bought some chocolates and a book. At about 2:00 p.m., she ran into a good friend of hers, Gladys King. King would later say that Dorothy seemed quite happy, in a good mood. Dorothy said she was going to take a walk through Central Park, and the two said good-bye. That was the last time anyone ever saw Dorothy. Central Park was filled with people, even on a chilly day, so she wouldn't have been alone. And yet, no trace of her could be found later on.

When Arnold didn't come home that day, her parents obviously became worried. They decided not to call the police to avoid a social scandal, which was a mistake that may have cost them valuable time.

Instead, they had their friend and lawyer, John Keith, look into the matter, but Keith couldn't find anything. All of Dorothy's clothes and possessions were still at home, which meant she had probably been kidnapped. She had a boyfriend at the time, a man her parents didn't like because he was older than her. But he was in Italy at the time of the disappearance, and knew nothing about it.

Keith searched all the morgues and hospitals, but found nothing. The family hired a private detective, but he also came up empty and told them they needed to contact the police, which they finally did in January 1911. The family also held a press conference and offered a reward for any information about her. They did receive two ransom notes, claiming that she had been kidnapped and demanding $5,000, but these turned out to be hoaxes. In February, the family received a postcard with the message

"I am safe" and Dorothy's signature, but no other information, and the signature looked like it might have been a copy.

Various others confessed to knowing where Dorothy was, or even being responsible for her death, but these always turned out to be false leads. She was never found. Somehow, a wealthy and well-known young woman managed to vanish without a trace in the middle of a busy city park on a typical afternoon, and no one had any idea what happened to her.

ANNA FELLOWS

Anna Fellows seemed to be happy enough. Born Anna Moran, she married William B. Fellows in 1876, and they lived in Massachusetts.

For three years, everything seemed to be going great. But in 1879, something happened. Mr. Fellows returned home one day to find Anna gone. She had apparently left him, but she left no note, no explanation. Of course, he began to search for her, but years passed, and he was never able to find her.

He'd long given up on ever seeing her again, when he came home one day in 1900 to find Anna in the kitchen, making dinner! It was as if nothing had happened. William had no idea what to make of it, and decided not to push Anna for an explanation. In any case, she never offered to tell him why she had been gone, or where she had been. So, they settled back into married life, and everything once again seemed to be going well, until 1903.

Once again, Anna vanished, and this time, she never came back. In 1926, reporters from Cambridge spoke to William (then about seventy years old), who told them this sad and strange story. Twice Anna had left him, and after the second instance, he never saw her again.

This story seems to border on being an urban legend, and, indeed, the further back in time you go, the harder it is to prove that such a story really happened. Elements of it are similar to British and Irish fairy lore: a fairy woman falls in love with a human, but is only able to spend a certain amount of time with him before she must go. She goes away without explanation, and maybe returns at some point in the future, or maybe goes back to her own world, where only a few days seem to have passed, but in our reality, many years have gone by.

It's very possible that this story is just made up. But what if it's true? Where did Anna go? Why did she stay away so long? Why was William happy not to ask her about where she'd been? What if she was actually a fairy, living in a world that was too modern for her? What if she only intended to go back to her realm for one night, but got caught up in a time loop, and came back to find that twenty-one years had passed?

THE SODDER CHILDREN

On Christmas Day in 1945, a horrible tragedy struck a family in the town of Fayetteville, West Virginia. George and Jennie Sodder's home burned down, and five of their nine children died in the fire. Or did they? The remains of these five children, Maurice, Martha, Louis, Jennie, and Betty, were never found in the ashes of the ruined house. And before their mysterious apparent disappearance in those early hours, some odd things had happened.

On Christmas Eve, the children had gone to bed as usual. But at about 12:30 a.m., the elder Jennie Sodder was awakened by the phone ringing. When she answered, she could hear a voice asking for someone she didn't know. She also heard glasses clinking in the background, and what she said was "weird laughter." After checking on the children, she went back to sleep, but was awakened again at about 1:00 a.m. by the sounds of an object hitting the roof, a loud bang, and something rolling. Surprisingly, she fell back asleep again. She was woken up one more time, at around 1:30 a.m., to the smell of smoke.

She woke up George, and they managed to get four children out of the house, but the passage to the attic level, where the other children were sleeping, was now blocked.

They sent one of the children to phone the fire department, while George went to get a ladder to climb to the window leading to the attic. But the ladder was missing. Even worse, both of his trucks wouldn't start, and no one was answering at the fire department, which in those days was all volunteer, with many firemen away fighting in World War II. Because of this, unfortunately, the firefighters only arrived in the morning, long after the fire had destroyed the house.

When the fire was investigated, they discovered the mystery. There were no remains for any of the five children still in the house. The fire had burned the house in less than an hour, not enough time to consume human bodies. The missing ladder was found hidden nearby. The fire department said it had been an electrical fire, but the family's Christmas lights were still on after the fire started, and they would have gone out if there had been an electrical short. Plus, their telephone wire had been cut (this was long before cell phones).

Others claimed they saw the five children in another car that night. It seemed like someone may have used the ladder to get up to the window, abduct the children, and then start a fire. But why?

A couple of months earlier, an insurance salesman had tried to sell George a policy, but he refused. The salesman became angry, and told him that his house would go up in smoke. He also warned George that he would pay for making "dirty remarks" about Mussolini, the dictator who had fought the Allies in World War II. In this community of Italian immigrants, some still supported him, even after he died. Another man had wanted to fix the fuse boxes in the house, warning George that they might catch fire, but George didn't hire him for the job.

The family began to think that the children had been kidnapped, perhaps by an organized crime group, though they never received any ransom notes. They never saw the children again, if they still lived, though in 1967, Jennie received a photo in the mail of a young man who could have

been Louis. But she was never able to get any more information. Whatever happened to them is still unknown.

A COLLECTION OF BRIEF BUT MYSTERIOUS DISAPPEARANCES

Sometimes, a story doesn't have a lot of details, or even need them; it's just weird and unexplainable. Here is a short list of some truly baffling disappearances that have never been solved. Charles Austin lived with his wife in Yonkers, New York. On March 28, 1905, he told her that he needed to step out for a bit, and to keep supper ready for him. She did so, and expected him back at any time. But he never returned, nor did he ever turn up anywhere else. There were no signs that anything was wrong, or that he was the victim of a crime; he just vanished without a trace. Ten years later, his wife gave up and had him declared legally dead.

In August 1880, a young man named Henry Edward was aboard a steamer ship, the *City of Dallas*, off the coast of Florida. It was a quiet night and the water was calm, and several crewmen were awake, including a night watch. Somehow, overnight, Edward disappeared.

The watch said they heard and saw nothing; a splash into the water would have been very noticeable, so it was unlikely that Edward just jumped in. He was never seen again, and no one knows what happened to him.

Andrew Carnegie Whitfield was a wealthy young man and an experienced pilot. On April 17, 1938, he took off in his small plane from Roosevelt Field on Long Island, headed for another airport only twenty-two miles away. It should have taken him about fifteen minutes, but neither he nor his plane ever arrived. A telephone operator reported that he had called while being searched for, and said he was going to carry out his plan. The official report concluded that he killed himself by flying into the Atlantic Ocean, but no wreckage was ever found, and he didn't seem to be in any trouble. Despite a few reported sightings of him in the years after, no proof was ever found.

William McKeekin was an engineer in New Jersey who was married on the Fourth of July, 1906. After the wedding ceremony, he told his new bride he was going to get a carriage for them. She excitedly waited for his return...which never happened. McKeekin vanished, as if he'd been whisked off the earth, as is so often the case in these strange accounts. His new bride searched for him for seventeen years before finally giving up.

James Regan was a passenger on the ship *Prinz Heinrich*, which was sailing from Marseilles on the south coast of France to Naples on the west coast of Italy in January 1914. It was a relatively short and uneventful trip, but somehow Regan disappeared. With all his luggage. In the middle of the voyage. No one could explain why, and he was never heard from again.

THE LINDBERGH BABY

On March 1, 1932, at around 10:00 p.m., Betty Gow, a nurse for Anne and Charles Lindbergh, found that ten-month-old Charles Augustus Lindbergh Jr. was missing from his crib. After a quick search by the Lindberghs and their staff, a ransom note was found in the child's room, as well as pieces of a broken ladder outside the window. New Jersey police found no fingerprints from the suspect and, after analyzing the ransom note, determined the kidnapper was most likely German because of the poor grammar in the note.

The kidnapping made national news, and due to the number of people who came to the Lindbergh home shortly after the kidnapping, any footprint evidence was destroyed. The Lindberghs and law enforcement initially believed the kidnapping was connected to organized crime, and even enlisted the help of Mob figures, including Al Capone, for help identifying the kidnapper. On March 6, the Lindberghs received two more ransom letters, which raised the ransom to $70,000 and were postmarked from Brooklyn. The kidnapper named James Condon, a retired Bronx schoolteacher, as intermediary between the kidnapper and the Lindberghs. On April 2, Condon passed along $50,000 in ransom to the alleged kidnapper, who told Condon that the baby was with two innocent women.

However, on May 12, a delivery truck driver found the body of a toddler who was quickly identified as Charles Jr., and who was cremated at the insistence of Lindbergh Sr. Investigators started to believe the perpetrator was someone the Lindberghs knew and began to suspect Violet Sharp, a servant at the home, who died by suicide after the police continued to harass her; after her death, her alibi was confirmed.

Eventually, the ransom money was tracked back to Richard Hauptmann, a German immigrant with a criminal record. He was arrested and interrogated by police. He insisted on his innocence even when investigators found several damning pieces of evidence that linked him to the case. Hauptmann was convicted of murder and maintained that he was innocent until his execution. After Hauptmann's execution, reporters and independent investigators began to question the way in which Hauptmann was arrested and the subsequent trial, and many began to believe that police had tampered with evidence to point to Hauptmann.

The kidnapping was considered to be one of the "trials of the century," and was regarded as "the biggest story since the Resurrection" at the time. This case inspired the Federal Kidnapping Act, also known as the "Little Lindbergh Law," which made transporting a kidnapped person across state lines a federal offense.

VANISHING IN FRONT OF OTHERS

There are several weird tales of people seeming to disappear right in front of others, making these instances the most mysterious stories of all.

A farmer named Orion Williamson left his house one day in July 1854 to go across a field and tell a hand about his horses. His family watched him from the porch, and some passing neighbors greeted him as he made his way out into the field. Then he just...vanished.

People were looking right at him one moment, and the next, he wasn't there. Locals searched but couldn't find Williamson anywhere.

It was if he'd just evaporated.

Years later, in September 1880, another farmer, David Lang, was walking across one of his fields near Gallatin, Tennessee, in full view of his family and some visitors, when he also vanished right before their eyes. A search of his field didn't turn up anything, and people even looked for places he might have fallen into, like hidden caves or sinkholes. But they found nothing.

Both of these tales are bizarre, but there is a problem with them. The first was told in a short story by the 19th-century author Ambrose Bierce, and who's to say he didn't just make it up? He might not have been telling a story he'd heard, but was instead inventing a chilling new tale for his readers. Likewise, when some people did research into the Lang case, they found no evidence that a man of that name had ever lived in Gallatin. So, was the Lang version just an urban legend, one based on Williamson's story? It's possible. And it's also possible that the Williamson story, if Bierce didn't invent it, was a local urban legend itself that spread around, in which the details were changed as needed.

So, as weird as these stories are, we don't have any way of confirming whether they actually happened. And they weren't the only ones.

There are several tales of someone going out to get water from a well and not returning. In one version, a boy's footprints end in snow, with no sign of anything around them, as if he were picked up. In other versions, the person getting the water is heard to cry out for help, and then is gone, but also with footprints vanishing at a certain point, as if the person were lifted up—perhaps an early UFO abduction?

These stories are hard to confirm, though. They may just be different versions of a local legend that got circulated to different areas. There is one genuine mystery, however. Ambrose Bierce went to Mexico in late 1913, when the country was in the middle of a turbulent revolution. Bierce vanished without a trace, leaving no evidence of what happened to him. Most think he must have been killed in the violence that was happening there, but no one knows for sure.

Like the field farmers, he was just gone. Only this time, we know it really happened!

OWEN PARFITT

Owen Parfitt had quite a history. At least, that's what he said. In his youth, he'd been involved in sailing, smuggling, and piracy, and even dabbled in black magic, but he'd become an old man with rheumatism. He was so crippled with disease that he could hardly walk or do anything for himself. And so, his sister let him live out his days at her country cottage near Shepton Mallet in Somerset, England. It was a comfortable life, but perhaps not the one Parfitt was used to, if he was telling the truth about his wild younger years.

One day in June 1763 (or possibly 1768, as reports differ), he was sitting on the front porch of the cottage, still in his nightclothes, as he had often done. Locals would sometimes come by and listen to his wild tales, and whether or not they believed him, he sure was entertaining! But on this fateful day, no one stopped by to see him.

His sister was out, and his caretaker, a young woman named Susannah Snook, had finished her duties and had left for the day. Sometime within a half hour or so of her leaving, she heard that he'd gone missing.

Susannah and Owen's sister searched far and wide, and had many others help them. They checked the woods and ponds and ditches, but there was no sign of him anywhere. The farms around their home had many workers and people, but no one had seen Owen. And this would have been impossible, anyway, because he could barely walk. Someone must have come and taken him away. But again, there were no signs of struggle, nothing was left behind except the coat he'd been wearing, and no neighbors had heard anything unusual.

He was just gone, as if he'd never existed. And if he'd been taken, who did it?

Rumors suggested that Parfitt's past life had caught up with him. Perhaps some old smugglers or other rivals had kidnapped him, taken him away, and killed him. Maybe they didn't want him talking about what he'd done in the old days. The more superstitious suggested that demons or evil spirits had come to collect him for a life of doing things he shouldn't have been doing.

But no one really knew what had happened.

A possible answer came fifty years later, when some work was done on a house nearby and a skeleton was dug up. Many thought this might be Parfitt, but they turned out to be the bones of a young woman, not an old man. To this day, every attempt to solve the mystery has failed, and no one knows what really happened to Owen Parfitt, or how he could have just vanished from the front of a cottage, in a populated area, without a trace.

ETTORE MAJORANA

Ettore Majorana was an Italian theoretical physicist who is the namesake for the Majorana equation and the Majorana fermions. From a young age, Majorana was extremely gifted in mathematics. He earned Laurea in physics from the University of Rome La Sapienza and published nine academic papers. Majorana was famous for not insisting on getting credit for his discoveries. In 1933 he went to Leipzig, Germany, on a grant from the National Research Council. When he returned to Rome in the fall, Majorana was ill from nervous exhaustion and acute gastritis. Due to his poor health, Majorana became more reclusive and shut himself away for four years. In 1938, he became a professor at the University of Naples, teaching theoretical physics.

Majorana traveled to Palermo, withdrawing all the money in his bank account, to visit his friend Emilio Segrè; however, Segrè was in California at the time. Majorana disappeared after purchasing a boat ticket from Palermo to Naples on March 25, 1938.

No investigations led to any clues about his fate. On the last day he was seen alive, Majorana sent the director of the Naples Physics Institute a letter apologizing for his sudden disappearance and thanking him for his friendship. The note did not allude to any plan, but did state that he would "keep a fond memory [of his students] at least until 11:00 p.m. tonight, possibly later too." Majorana also canceled his other travel plans through telegram and allegedly bought a ticket to Naples, but was never seen again.

While there is no official explanation for Majorana's disappearance, an investigation in 2015 led some to believe that Majorana had lived in Valencia, Venezuela, from 1955 to 1959. Due to new evidence, investigators officially closed the case and determined that Majorana most likely disappeared of his own volition, while some of his colleagues and friends believe he could have committed suicide, become a beggar, retired in a monastery, been murdered to prevent him from working on nuclear weapons, or emigrated to Argentina or Venezuela.

CHARLES E. BOLES, "BLACK BART"

Charles E. Boles, better known as Black Bart, was an American outlaw who was notorious for stagecoach robberies in Northern California and Oregon in the 1870s and 1880s.

Originally from England, Boles moved to Upstate New York as a toddler and eventually joined the California Gold Rush with two of his brothers. He later returned to the East Coast, where he served in the Civil War and married Mary Elizabeth Johnson, with whom he had four children. While searching for gold in Idaho and Montana in 1867, Boles had a bad encounter with agents working for Wells Fargo & Company and vowed to avenge the meeting.

From 1875 to 1883, Boles reportedly robbed twenty-eight stagecoaches in Northern California and became notorious for leaving poems at the site of his robberies. He was considered a "gentleman bandit" because of his good manners, his polite nature, his shotgun that he never used, and his clothing style: always wearing a linen duster coat, a bowler hat, and a flour sack over his head with holes for his eyes. After being wounded during a robbery, Boles fled and left behind several personal items that led to his arrest.

Wells Fargo only charged Boles for one robbery, and he served four years in San Quentin State Prison, being released two years early in January 1888 for good behavior. During his time in prison, his health had deteriorated, causing him to go deaf in one ear. After being released from prison, Boles wrote to his wife that he was tired of being followed by Wells Fargo and wished to disappear from the spotlight. He never returned to his family, but Wells Fargo traced him to Visalia, California, where he eventually disappeared.

The last sighting of Black Bart was February 28, 1888. Some theories on what happened to Boles after his disappearance included his becoming a pharmacist in Marysville, California, while Wells Fargo detectives believed he fled to Japan.

JOSEPH FORCE CRATER

The Joseph Force Crater case became a sensation in America in the early 1930s, and it remains one of the most high-profile missing persons cases ever. Crater was a judge on the New York Supreme Court, a successful lawyer, and a well-known figure in New York. He was appointed to his position in 1930 by Franklin Delano Roosevelt, who was governor of the state before going on to become president of the United States.

In early August 1930, Crater and his wife were vacationing in Maine. He told her on August 3 that he needed to return to New York City to do some business, but would be back as soon as he could.

This wasn't that unusual; judges are busy people. On the evening of August 6, Crater had dinner in New York with a lawyer friend named William Klein, and a Broadway performer named Sally Lou Ritz. They ate at a "chophouse" (an inexpensive steak restaurant), and then Crater left them to hail a taxi and go see a Broadway show, *Dancing Partner*. These two were among the last to report seeing him alive. Crater apparently never attended the play, and seemed to simply vanish.

An investigation was launched right away (a missing judge is a big deal), and more sinister and suspicious information came to light. It turned out that on the morning of August 6, Crater had destroyed some of his documents, moved others, and withdrew about $5,000 from his bank account (a lot of money in those days—over $75,000 in today's value). Also, it turned out that earlier in the year, he may have paid even more money to a corrupt organization, Tammany Hall, to basically "buy" the judge's position. So people started putting two and two together, and suspected that he had done something to anger someone, whether that someone was higher up or involved in organized crime, or whatnot. Perhaps the extra $5,000 was another bribe, an attempt to pay off and keep someone quiet? Or maybe Crater was in trouble for not ruling the way he was expected to on certain cases?

In any event, the investigation failed to turn up any trace of Crater, or anyone who had seen what had happened to him. He just disappeared.

For a high-profile judge to vanish so completely was unheard of, and some people began to think that maybe he "skipped town" and ran off with the money to start a new life somewhere else. But surely somebody would have recognized him at some time?

Another clue finally came to light in 2005. New York police revealed that an elderly woman, Stella Ferrucci-Good, had died that year and left a note saying that her police officer husband (also dead) had learned that another police officer named Charles Burns murdered Crater with the help of one other man, and buried him under the Coney Island boardwalk. It was related to organized crime. Unfortunately, there's no way to determine this now, and many are still skeptical.

It may be true, but there isn't any other evidence, so Crater's fate remains a mystery.

THE BLOODY BENDERS

The Benders were a family of serial killers from Labette County, Kansas. The family consisted of John and Elvira Bender and their children, John Jr. and Kate (although some newspapers claimed that John Jr. and Kate were in a common-law marriage).

In October 1870, the Bender family moved to the township of Osage and bought 160 acres of land, where they built a cabin, barn, and well. That's where they lived and opened a general store. It is believed that the Bender parents spoke very little English and were extremely unfriendly, while John Jr. and Kate regularly attended services at a nearby Sunday school. Kate was popular in town and was a self-proclaimed psychic and healer, professing she could cure illnesses and conduct seances. Kate also conducted lectures on spiritualism and allegedly claimed that murder was not inherently bad, and she was open about her incestuous relationship with her brother.

Beginning in the 1870s, several men were found dead and several more people went missing around Kansas. In March 1873, Colonel Alexander M. York went to the Benders' inn (the cabin where the Benders lived, operated a small general store, and offered a small place for travelers to eat and sleep) to investigate the disappearance of his brother. The Benders admitted that his brother had stayed at the inn but denied any involvement in his disappearance. A month later, York was informed that a woman had fled the Benders' inn after being threatened by Elvira. After York confronted Elvira, she became enraged and slipped up, revealing that she had a better grasp of English than she let on to community members.

Although investigators suspected the Benders, they continued to look into other leads and worked to get warrants to search houses in the neighborhood; this gave the Benders ample opportunity to flee, and three days later, community members noticed the inn had been abandoned. Investigators and volunteers began to search the Benders' property, where they found over ten bodies. A manhunt ensued for the capture of the four Benders, and while many claim to have found and killed them, no official identification was ever made.

THEODORE "TED" COLE AND RALPH ROE

Theodore Cole and Ralph Roe were convicted bank robbers from Oklahoma. After several independent escape attempts from Oklahoma State Penitentiary, both Cole and Roe were transferred to United States Penitentiary Leavenworth and eventually to Alcatraz, an "escape-proof" prison in San Francisco, California.

In Alcatraz, the pair got jobs working at the prison's mat shop, where inmates turned old car tires into rubber mats for the US Navy. On December 16, 1937, Cole and Roe were working in the mat shop when

a dense fog appeared through the San Francisco Bay, causing the visibility from Alcatraz to be almost zero and confusing marine traffic. Both Cole and Roe were accounted for at the 1:00 p.m. head count but had disappeared by the 1:30 p.m. head count. During the fog, the pair had cut a large hole in the shop's window and slipped out of the building. They then used a wrench to force the lock on the gate open and continued on to the beach, where investigators lost their trail.

After several days of investigation, guards found no evidence besides the wrench used to unlock the gate. It was revealed that the men had planned this escape attempt in advance by weakening the window bars with a hacksaw blade. It is believed that the pair used tires or fuel canisters as a makeshift raft once they arrived at the beach.

Alcatraz officials believe Cole and Roe drowned in the bay due to the 40–50 degree water, harsh ebb tides, and thick fog that was prevalent on the day and time of their escape. Although it is most likely that the pair were swept out into the Pacific Ocean and drowned, police departments and the FBI continued to follow tips from the public, which included two hitchhikers claiming to have seen the men shortly after their escape. The *San Francisco Chronicle* claimed the pair were alive and well in South America, and others from Cole's hometown of Seminole, Oklahoma, believed they returned there and resumed their crime spree.

THE LAKE ANJIKUNI MYSTERY

November 30, 1930, was a very cold day. A trapper named Joe Labelle was in northern Canada and needed shelter from the elements. He knew of an Inuit village next to Lake Anjikuni and decided he would go there. He'd been before, and it was warm and friendly—just the kind of place he needed to take shelter and rest. He went to the village expecting that kind of welcome, but none came. The village was completely empty.

Labelle searched around and found that clothing was still there, as were personal belongings, food, and much more. It was as if the whole village had been abandoned in a big hurry. At least thirty people should have been there, but there were none. He was too frightened to stay, so he managed to hike to an outpost, where he could send a message by telegraph. The Royal Canadian Mounted Police received his message and sent their own team to investigate.

It turned out that another trapper and his sons had been in the area near the lake, and claimed they had seen a mysterious light in the sky that seemed to be able to change shape.

The police searched the village and found another unsettling sight: several graves were disturbed, and the bodies had been removed.

This was something that Inuit people would never do, so whatever took them must have been an outsider.

The story was reported in some papers and was a genuine mystery before interest in it wore out and, like so many other strange tales, it was forgotten. In 1959, an author named Frank Edwards mentioned the story in his book *Stranger Than Science*, which attracted investigators again. As a result, the Canadian police started saying the event never happened— that Edwards had made it up. This was a particularly bizarre response, because newspaper reports of the event exist from 1930. Skeptics claim the stories from then were also made up, or at least exaggerated. It turned out that Labelle hadn't been an experienced outdoorsman at all, and he might have stumbled on a village that had been abandoned for the season, not permanently.

The other details were inventions, skeptics say.

But records exist that show the police did investigate the case, meaning they thought it was unusual, not a seasonal practice. And they admitted that it was very strange to leave behind food, clothing, and supplies. As a result, many think the police were covering up something they couldn't explain or that was too disturbing to report. Some believe the light in the sky might have been a UFO. Others think that the mythic Wendigo might have taken them. We don't know how much of the story is true and how much is made up; it's been too long, and if someone were trying to cover up part of the story, it would be hard now to figure out what it was. It seems like something terrible and unexpected did happen to the inhabitants of this village, but we'll probably never know the details.

JEAN-FRANÇOIS DE GALAUP, COMTE DE LAPÉROUSE

Jean-François de Galaup, comte de Lapérouse, often called Lapérouse, was a French explorer and naval officer. Lapérouse's family was ennobled in 1558, before Lapérouse was born in 1741. Lapérouse joined the French Navy in 1756, and was a part of several supply expeditions to Louisebourg in New France throughout the Seven Years' War. Lapérouse commanded a ship in the Anglo-French War in 1778. In 1783, Lapérouse's family allowed him to marry Louise-Eléonore Broudou, whom he met in present-day Mauritius. Louis XVI and the Secretary of State of the Navy appointed Lapérouse to lead a voyage around the world for scientific exploration.

Lapérouse's expedition was meant to conclude the discoveries of James Cook in the Pacific, which included completing maps, establishing trade contacts, finding new maritime routes, and collecting information to better the French scientific community. Lapérouse was given two ships, *L'Astrolabe* and *La Boussole.* Lapérouse's crew of 220 included ten scientists and two chaplains. The expedition went to Chile, Hawaii, Alaska, California, East Asia, Japan, Russia, Australia, and the South Pacific.

Lapérouse's crew arrived near Botany Bay on January 24, 1788, where they stayed with a British convoy led by Captain Arthur Phillip RN. The French and British officers visited each other on several occasions, and assisted each other and shared supplies. Lapérouse sent journals, scientific charts, and letters back to France through the British merchant ship *Alexander,* and his crew built an observatory and garden where they held mass and studied the geography of the area. On March 10, Lapérouse and his expedition left New South Wales to explore the western and southern coasts of Australia, and he sent a letter saying they should return to France in June 1789. But Lapérouse and his crew were never seen again (and it is believed that on the day of his execution, Louis XVI asked if there was any information about Lapérouse). Documents of Lapérouse's were published in 1791 in Paris, entitled *Voyage de La Pérouse autour du monde* (*The Voyage of La Pérouse around the world*).

A 1791 rescue mission turned up no leads on Lapérouse's expedition. During the French Revolution, there were rumors that Lapérouse was betrayed by the British, despite a lack of evidence. Around forty years later, it was discovered that Lapérouse's expedition was wrecked on a coral reef on a low island between New Caledonia and New Guinea. A British whaler went to the island and met with locals who had a cross of St. Louis's, medals from Louis XVI, and a sword with "Paris" written on it. A chief on the island said a ship had been wrecked when he was a child. According to evidence recovered in several expeditions, both ships wrecked on the reefs of Vanikoro, and some survivors were killed by local inhabitants. Some islanders claimed that a group of the surviving sailors created a small ship made from the wreckage of *L'Astrolabe* and sailed west, but their fate is ultimately unknown. It is also believed that two men stayed behind but left the island a few years before the first rescue mission.

The La Perouse suburb in New South Wales was named after Lapérouse, as are several other locations in Alaska, Hawaii, British Columbia, Vancouver, Australia, New Zealand, and Easter Island, and even a crater on the moon. Lapérouse was also the namesake of a few ships and was mentioned in *Twenty Thousand Leagues Under the Sea* by Jules Verne, the television series *Northern Exposure, Walden* by Henry David Thoreau, and an opera composed by Jon Appleton.

ALICE KYTELER

Alice Kyteler was the first recorded woman to be condemned for witchcraft in Ireland. Kyteler was the only daughter of a Flemish family that settled in County Kilkenny, Ireland. Kyteler was married four times: to William Outlaw (a wealthy merchant, moneylender, and mayor of Kilkenny), Adam Blund (a moneylender), Richard de Valle (a wealthy landowner), and John le Poer. In 1302, Kyteler and Blund were accused of killing Outlaw. Le Poer defended her but soon fell ill, with many believing that he was being poisoned. After le Poer passed away, Kyteler's stepchildren from all three former husbands accused her of poisoning their fathers, as well as using sorcery.

Kyteler was charged with seven formal crimes: denying the power of Christ and the Church, sacrificing animals to demons, asking demons for advice on witchcraft, having a sexual relationship with a demon, holding coven meetings, making dark-magic powders, and killing her husbands. Le Poer was the only husband to raise suspicion against Kyteler while they were alive, and before he passed, his will was edited to give more financial benefit to Kyteler and first-born son, with William Outlaw, rather than the children from his previous marriage.

It is believed that Kyteler likely killed at least one of her husbands, and their children accused her of witchcraft in order to secure a conviction, as witchcraft was more taboo than murder at that time. Kyteler's motives for killing her husbands are uncertain, but it is believed that it could have been to obtain the wealth they possessed, or that she was unsatisfied sexually in marriage, and the patriarchal values in Ireland restrained her from being happy.

Kyteler was arrested, along with her servant, Petronilla de Meath, de Meath's daughter, Basilia, and at least ten other people. Before Kyteler could be sentenced by the court and the church, she and Basilia escaped. De Meath was flogged and burned to death, and William Outlaw was excommunicated and imprisoned until he begged for forgiveness. Kyteler and Basilia were never seen or heard from again. Kyteler and her followers were the first people to be accused of witchcraft in Ireland, and their cases set a precedent of burning those accused of witchcraft that would last until 1895.

BARBARA NEWHALL FOLLETT

Barbara Newhall Follett was an American child prodigy and novelist who went missing in 1939, when she was twenty-five years old. Follett was born in New Hampshire to literary editor and critic Wilson Follett and children's author Helen Thomas Follett. Follett was schooled at home by her mother and began writing her own poetry at age four. At seven, Follett was writing about an imaginary world, Farksolia, and developing its own language, Farksoo.

When she was eight years old, Follett began writing a book that would later become *The House Without Windows*, which was published with help from her father in 1927. The book was met with critical acclaim and Barbara was deemed a child genius. In 1928, she published her second book, *The Voyage of the Norman D.*, which was also met with critical acclaim. When Follett was sixteen, her father left the family for another woman and her family fell victim to the Great Depression, so she was forced to take a job as a secretary in New York City. Follett married Nickerson Rogers in 1934 and began to express signs of depression in 1937 and 1938, when she began to fear Rogers was unfaithful and publishers no longer wanted her manuscripts.

According to Rogers, Follett left their apartment in Brookline, Massachusetts, on December 7, 1939, with $30 after a fight. Rogers did not report her disappearance to police for two weeks, stating that he believed she would return. He waited four months to request a missing persons bulletin, which he filed under her married name, so the media did not learn of her disappearance until 1966, when Follett's mother, Helen, coauthored an academic study on Follett and her strange disappearance.

Helen had become suspicious of Rogers, and, in 1952, demanded that Brookline police investigate her daughter's disappearance again. In 1948, a deer hunter had come across human remains in the woods of Mount Prospect in New Hampshire; the skeleton was attributed to another missing woman, Elsie Whittemore, but there were several discrepancies that led many internet sleuths to believe that they could have been Follett's remains: for instance, finding horn-rimmed glasses near the body that matched the style Follett was known to wear, the location being near the family of Follett, and the body's height and shoe size being similar to Follett's. However, the remains were never confirmed to be either woman. Barbara's body (or any trace of her) was never discovered.

SOLOMON NORTHUP

Solomon Northup was an American abolitionist best known for being the primary author of the memoir *Twelve Years a Slave.* Northup was born in the early 1800s to a free woman of color and a freedman. Thus, he and his brother, Joseph, were born free in New York. Northup and his brother grew up working on the family farm, and he spent his free time reading and playing the violin. Northup married Anne Hampton in 1829, shortly after his father died, and they lived together at Fort House in Washington County, New York, and later moved to Sandy Hill.

In 1841, when Northup was thirty-two years old, he met two men who claimed to be members of a circus company. The men, who introduced themselves as Merrill Brown and Abram Hamilton, offered him a job as a fiddler. Northup, who believed the trip would be brief, did not notify his family that he was working. The men persuaded Northup to accompany them to Washington, D.C., which, at the time, had one of the US's largest slave markets. People would often kidnap free Black people and sell them into the slave trade. It is believed that Brown and Hamilton incapacitated Northup and sold him to slave trader James H. Birch under the guise that Northup was a fugitive slave. Northup was then taken to New Orleans through the coastwise slave trade. Northup was able to convince an English sailor to send a letter to Henry B. Northup, a lawyer who was related to the man who freed Northup's father. While enslaved, Northup was sold to several men in Louisiana and suffered cruel treatment and beatings.

In 1852, Northup confided in Canadian carpenter and abolitionist Samuel Bass his true identity, making Bass the only person Northup had told his secret to during his time as a slave. Bass assisted in contacting Northup's family, friends, and former employers in an effort to help Northup escape. While it was illegal to assist slaves under a congressional act, the New York State Legislature passed a law in 1840 that made it illegal to kidnap an African American out of New York and sell them into slavery. When Anne learned of Northup's kidnapping, she had a deposition with the Justice of the Peace and prepared a letter to the governor of New York, Washington Hunt, to gather information that Northup was free.

Northup returned to his family on January 21, 1853. After he came home, Northup wrote and published his memoir, *Twelve Years a Slave*, which documented his kidnapping and treatment as a slave. Northup was traumatized after his time in slavery and was said to be drunk often. It is unknown what happened to Northup, as he was not listed in the 1860 census (along with his family), but his wife was identified as a widow by 1875.

JEAN SPANGLER

Jean Spangler was an American actress who disappeared in 1949. Originally from Seattle, Spangler graduated from Franklin High School in Los Angeles, California, and was a dancer in the Earl Carroll Theatre. She also began appearing as a dancer in small, uncredited roles in Hollywood films. Spangler married Dexter Benner in 1942, and they divorced four years later. At the time she went missing, Spangler was living with her daughter, Christine, her mother, her brother, and her sister-in-law, Sophie, in the Park La Brea residential complex near Wilshire Boulevard.

On October 7, 1949, Spangler left Christine with Sophie and went out around 5:00 p.m. She stated that she was meeting with Benner to discuss child support and then was going to work on a night shoot. Approximately two hours later, Spangler called her home and spoke to both Sophie and Christine, saying that she would have to work late and would not return home that evening. The next morning, Sophie filed a missing persons

report when Spangler did not return home. Police reached out to Hollywood studios and the Screen Extras Guild to see where Spangler was working, but they had no record of Spangler working that night. A saleswoman at the Farmers Market at the corner of Fairfax Avenue and Third Street in Los Angeles recalled that she had seen Spangler shopping around 6:00 p.m., and she appeared to be waiting for someone. Benner and his new wife stated that they had not heard from Spangler for several weeks.

On October 9, Spangler's purse was found in Griffith Park near the Fern Dell entrance, which was about five miles from her home. The straps of her purse were torn, as if someone had ripped it from her arm. Police and volunteers searched the park and found no other pieces of evidence connected to Spangler, but a dog dug up a Los Angeles County Jail uniform. The purse had no money, but Sophie stated that Spangler didn't have any money when she left the house.

Inside the purse there was a note that read "Kirk: Can't wait any longer, Going to see Dr. Scott. It will work best this way while mother is away." Spangler's mother, Florence, was visiting family in Kentucky at the time. Florence told police that a man named Kirk had picked up Spangler twice but had not come inside. Police were unable to find a Dr. Scott with Spangler as a patient, but Spangler was once in an abusive relationship with a man named Scotty, though they had not been in contact since 1945. At the time she went missing, Spangler had just finished filming *Young Man with a Horn*, starring Kirk Douglas, leading to speculation that he was the Kirk referred to in the note. Douglas originally denied knowing Spangler but later admitted to talking to her on set, though he claimed he had never met with her outside work.

Spangler's friends told police she was three months pregnant at the time of her disappearance and had discussed getting an illegal abortion. Spangler also told her friend that she was having an affair but it was not serious. Several theories have come out about Spangler's disappearance, including Spangler being linked to the Black Dahlia murder.

Allegedly, Spangler was seen with Davy Ogul, an associate of American mobster Mickey Cohen, in Las Vegas and Palm Springs. Ogul went missing two days after Spangler, presumably to escape prosecution for conspiracy. A customs agent in El Paso, Texas, reported seeing Ogul and a woman that looked like Spangler in 1950, but Spangler's sister claims Spangler was never acquainted with Ogul. The Los Angeles Police Department has not closed the case, and Spangler is still considered a missing person.

GRAND DUCHESS ANASTASIA NIKOLAEVNA OF RUSSIA

Anastasia Nikolaevna was the fourth daughter of Tsar Nicholas II and Tsarina Alexandra, born in June 1901 to the Romanov Russian Imperial family. Anastasia was described as lively, mischievous, and daring, and was known for playing pranks that often went too far.

During the Russian Revolution in February 1917, the Romanov family was put under house arrest at the Alexander Palace. Tsar Nicolas II abdicated the throne on March 15. As the Bolsheviks, a Marxist group founded by Vladimir Lenin, approached the palace, Alexander Kerensky of the Provisional Government had the family moved to Tobolsk, Siberia. The Romanovs were moved to the Ipatiev House in Yekaterinburg after the Bolsheviks took control of the majority of Russia.

While in captivity, the family was kept in isolation and had to follow strict rules that included only speaking in Russian, ringing a bell whenever they wanted to leave their rooms, and employing servants who were meant to only address the family by their names, not their titles. The house was surrounded by a thirteen-foot-tall defensive wall, and the windows were sealed shut and covered with newspaper. The family was constantly searched, was denied from attending church, did not receive the newspaper, and was watched by 300 guards. A machine gun was pointed at the bedroom of the tsar and tsarina.

After the Bolshevik revolution ended in November 1917, the country quickly fell apart as it entered the Russian Civil War. The Romanovs' extended family, many of whom were a part of the royal houses of Europe, attempted to negotiate with the Bolsheviks for the release of the family. Anti-Bolshevik forces, referred to as the Whites, approached Yekaterinburg and were on the verge of taking the city. When the White Army reached Yekaterinburg, they found that the Romanovs had disappeared.

According to the account of Yakov Yurovsky—the head of the detachment watching the Romanovs—that was recovered in 1989, he led a group of Bolshevik secret police to execute Tsar Nicholas II and his family on the night of July 16, 1918. Yurovsky instructed the family to wait in the basement and told Nicholas II that he was to be executed. The guard shot and killed Nicholas II, Alexandra, and their five children, Olga, Tatiana, Maria, Anastasia, and Alexei, as well as four members of the imperial entourage. When disposing of the bodies, the drunken Bolsheviks looted them, as the women had sewn diamonds into their undergarments. The bodies had been dumped in a mineshaft but were subsequently moved several times after being dismembered and covered in acid in order to prevent identification.

Throughout the 20th century, many believed that Anastasia had escaped her family's fate. Over the years, several women claimed to be Anastasia, the most famous of which was Anna Anderson. Anderson claimed around 1920 that she was Anastasia and had pretended to be dead and was rescued by a sympathetic soldier. Anderson attempted a legal battle in Germany from 1938 to 1970 for recognition of her identity, but was denied by the court. After her death, Anderson's DNA was compared to the blood of Prince Philip, Duke of Edinburgh, the great-nephew of Empress Alexandra, and Anderson was found to be an impostor.

Immediately after the execution, Soviet leadership gave several answers to the fate of the Romanovs, but finally acknowledged the murders in 1926. In 1979, Alexander Avdonin, an amateur sleuth, found the family's remains, and the Soviet Union acknowledged them publicly in 1989. By 2007, the bodies of all family members were discovered, confirming they had all died in 1918.

CHAPTER 2
INTO THIN AIR

FLYING DOESN'T COME NATURALLY to humans. In our history, it wasn't until relatively recently that we managed to get off the ground. Many people are afraid of flying, and those of us who aren't likely still feel a little burst of nerves (excitement, anticipation, call it what you will) at takeoff. Usually, there's not much merit to these worries. As aviation evolves, it gets safer and more reliable. But there may be something to that feeling of trepidation. There are times that planes take off and never seem to touch back down again, lost in the vast expanse of sky that is so foreign to us. What mysterious forces may be at work in the sky and space above? This chapter includes the stories of those who may have learned the answer to that question, but never got the chance to reveal it.

AMELIA EARHART

Amelia Earhart's is one of the most famous disappearances in history. Countless books, articles, movies, and TV shows have tried to figure out what happened to her, an experienced and decorated pilot whose plane vanished over the Pacific Ocean in 1937.

She was an amazing aviator who was the first woman to make a solo flight across the Atlantic Ocean, as well as the first person to complete a solo flight from Hawaii to the US mainland. In light of these accomplishments, her disappearance during another long flight is not as straightforward as you might assume.

On March 17, 1937, Earhart and navigator Fred Noonan took off from Oakland, California, in an attempt to fly around the world, making several stops along the way, of course. But something went wrong and the plane suffered damage, so it took time to be repaired.

Finally, they were ready again, and flew to Miami, Florida. On June 1, they flew from Florida to South America, before crossing the Atlantic and flying to Africa. From there, they journeyed on to India and then Southeast Asia. They reached New Guinea on June 29. They'd flown over 22,000 miles and only had another 7,000 miles to go to return to Oakland.

They left on July 2, heading for a tiny spot of land called Howland Island, about halfway between Australia and Hawaii. They planned to land there to refuel. At the time, a US Coast Guard ship was anchored there. Along the way, Earhart and Noonan lost radio contact with the ship. They were never seen again. A massive search over the following few weeks turned up nothing. They were declared lost at sea, and the plane was assumed to have crashed into the vast Pacific Ocean, where it would never be found.

How could such an experienced pilot have lost control and crashed, if that's what really happened? That portion of the flight turned out to have several problems. To make room for more fuel, they left behind some of their radio equipment, and the weather conditions were not good. Also, the map they had to Howland Island may have been wrong, putting the island several miles away from where it actually was.

It was long thought that Earhart and Noonan had simply vanished into the ocean, but in recent years, some intriguing information has come to light. Some now think they were able to land on Nikumaroro Reef, another small island 350 miles southeast of Howland Island.

Investigations there have turned up some interesting finds, including a woman's shoe, some Plexiglas from a window, a jar of cosmetic cream, and a scrap of metal that might have belonged to the plane.

Radio transmissions were also picked up as far away as San Francisco and even Canada. One said, "Still alive. Better hurry. Tell husband all right." Another, amazingly, said, "Can you read me? This is Amelia Earhart.... Please come in."

It seems that Earhart (and maybe Noonan) was able to survive for days or even weeks after landing on Nikumaroro, but eventually ran out of food and water before anyone could find them. If this is true, it's a tragic end for one of the greatest pilots of the 20th century.

LIEUTENANT FELIX MONCLA AND RADAR OBSERVER R. R. WILSON

On the evening of November 23, 1953, the US Air Force Defense Command picked up something strange on radar.

A genuine UFO seemed to be flying over Lake Superior at about 500 miles per hour. That was more than enough to cause alarm, as it could have been a Soviet jet or something else. An F-89C all-weather jet was scrambled from nearby Kinross Air Force Base in Michigan to intercept the object and find out what it was. Lt. Felix Moncla, a skilled airman with over 800 hours of flying experience, was piloting it. The second crewman was the radar observer, Second Lieutenant R. R. Wilson.

Back at the base, the radar operator gave Moncla instructions to come down from an altitude of 25,000 feet to about 7,000 feet, where the object was. He watched the two objects on radar. Moncla's jet got closer and closer; then the two objects seemed to "merge" on the radar screen. The operator assumed that Moncla had flown over or under the UFO and would show up in front of it in a few seconds.

But he never did. The other object just kept going on its original course, before eventually veering off and also disappearing from radar.

Somehow, Moncla's jet had simply vanished from existence. The Air Force conducted an extensive search, but found no trace of the jet or the crewmen in the waters or on shore. The Air Force then released an official report confirming that the jet and the unknown object had merged and the jet had vanished. This story was run in newspapers, but, as you can probably already imagine, the Air Force backed up and changed its story soon after, just as it had done with Roswell (the site of an infamous suspected UFO incident in 1947). It then claimed that Moncla had completed his mission, and identified the UFO as a plane from Canada that had gotten off course. After that, they said, he had suffered from vertigo (motion sickness), lost control of the jet, and crashed into the lake. Then they changed the story again, and said the jet had exploded at a higher altitude. If this is sounding ridiculous to you, a lot of other people thought so too!

In fact, Canadian officials said that none of their planes had been in the area that night. So clearly, someone wasn't telling the truth, and it was starting to sound like the guilty party was the US Air Force....

Obviously, the Air Force changed its story more than once, probably because it couldn't explain what had happened. Even more interesting, investigators from the National Investigations Committee on Aerial Phenomena (NICAP) found out that all descriptions of Moncla's mission had been removed from the official records. Clearly, someone was trying to hide something.

To this day, no one knows for sure what happened. UFO enthusiasts believe the entire jet may have been taken aboard an alien ship, which is why radar showed them merging. In 1968, there were reports of jet wreckage in Lake Superior, but no one ever confirmed this. In 2006, an investigator claimed to have found parts of the jet, as well as a portion of an unknown craft, unlike anything on earth, but this story seemed to be a hoax, and the person that made it up has since disappeared. Were Moncla and Wilson taken aboard an alien spacecraft? If so, what happened to them, and why were they never brought back?

FREDERICK VALENTICH

On October 21, 1978, a young pilot named Frederick Valentich departed from just south and west of Melbourne, Australia, on a training flight, and headed over the ocean out to King Island, off the south coast of Australia. All was going fine until just after 7:00 p.m., when he radioed the Melbourne Flight Service, saying that a UFO was pursuing his small Cessna airplane. The flight service told him that no other aircraft were in the area, but he insisted that something with four landing lights was directly above him and moving at a good speed. If it was, then it wasn't showing up on radar.

Five minutes later, Valentich reported that the craft had gotten nearer to him and was almost "orbiting" him. He felt like whoever or whatever was in the UFO was messing with him, and not necessarily in a playful way. He said it seemed to be a metallic, shiny object, and he could see a green light on it. The flight service again confirmed that no aircraft other than his was in the area.

Then it vanished, only to reappear soon. Valentich confirmed that he was flying to King Island and then said that he was having engine trouble—that the engine was "coughing." He said the mysterious object was hovering above him again, and that it was not an aircraft, meaning it didn't look like any known plane. Those were his last words. Seventeen seconds of silence followed, then what sounded like a scraping sound before the radio went dead.

The first thought was that he'd had engine trouble, the engine had given out, and he'd crashed into the sea. A search and rescue mission was mounted to scout the air and ocean, but they found no trace of Valentich or his plane. It seemed like he had just vanished, that something had taken him and maybe even his plane. Did an alien craft abduct him?

About five years later, a piece of engine from the same kind of plane washed up on another nearby island, but investigators weren't able to determine if it was from Valentich's Cessna. Skeptics pointed out that Valentich was a strong believer in UFOs and aliens and that he actually worried about being attacked by one while flying. Also, they said he was not experienced as a pilot, and had failed twice in trying to join the Air Force, and twice in trying to become a commercial pilot. He was clearly not as good at it as he wanted to be. This inexperience, combined with his belief in alien ships, they said, meant that he probably was confused, saw some other lights, and panicked, keeping him from being able to manage when the genuine engine trouble arose. He lost control, and the plane fell into the sea.

Not so fast, say some UFO researchers. They point out that there were other reports of strange lights in the sky in the same area that night, especially green ones like Valentich said he saw. According to an unconfirmed report, a farmer saw a large (ninety feet or so) UFO hovering over his land the morning after, and he could see a small airplane stuck to the side of it, leaking oil. This is an amazing claim, but so far, no one has been able to prove whether it's true.

The mystery of Valentich's disappearance is still in question. Did an alien ship take him and his plane right out of the sky? Why? And what happened to him if it did?

DAN (D. B.) COOPER, THE MYSTERY HIJACKER

On the afternoon of November 24, 1971, a man calling himself Dan Cooper bought a one-way plane ticket from Portland to Seattle.

He wore a black suit and tie and a white shirt, as well as dark sunglasses. He sat quietly on the plane, until after it took off. At about 3:00 p.m., he handed one of the flight attendants a note, which said that he had a bomb in his briefcase and that he wanted her to sit next to him. Obviously afraid, she did, and he opened his briefcase to show her what looked like a mess of dynamite and wires.

He wrote a new note and told her to take it to the pilot. The note demanded that, after landing in Seattle, he be provided with parachutes and $200,000 in cash. After the plane landed, he allowed the passengers to leave, but kept the crew and pilots on board while waiting for his demands to be met. The money and parachutes were brought, the plane was refueled, and he told them to fly to Mexico City. The plane took off again in the evening, headed south.

But then, Cooper did something unexpected. As the plane neared the Washington/Oregon border, he put on one of the parachutes, took the money, and jumped out of the plane. The crew was not even aware of it until sometime later. He either had no intention of going all the way to Mexico City, or had changed his mind and decided to bail out sooner.

Obviously, a search began almost immediately, but Cooper was nowhere to be found. Most people seem to think he died in the jump or the landing, and his body was never found, seemingly lost in the wilderness north of Portland. But this explanation has many problems. Cooper clearly had a good knowledge of flights, planes, and parachuting. He obviously knew what he was doing, so it seems unlikely that he panicked and jumped sooner than he intended. On the other hand, the area he jumped into was pretty rugged and rough, and it would have been difficult, even for an experienced parachuter, to make a jump like that, in the dark, freezing cold, and in unfamiliar land, to a designated landing site.

Some of the money was later found near the Columbia River, which again led many to assume that Cooper had died trying to escape. But not all the money was there, and still, there was no trace of Cooper anywhere. The FBI rounded up a large list of possible suspects, but one by one, they eliminated these men. Today, we still don't know who "Dan Cooper" really was, or what happened to him. The FBI stopped work on the case in 2016, but still invites local law enforcement and amateur sleuths to come forward with any new evidence they've uncovered.

The fact is that a man calling himself Dan Cooper hijacked a plane, took a large amount of money, and disappeared, never to be seen again. As with so many of these stories, it was as if he'd just vanished off the face of the earth.

THE BERMUDA TRIANGLE: A LOST FLIGHT

The Bermuda Triangle is, without a doubt, the most famous "mysterious" place in the world. There have been countless tales of disappearances in this strange area, which covers mostly ocean between the southeast tip of Florida down to Puerto Rico and up to the tiny island of Bermuda. In this area, an unknown number of ships and airplanes are said to have vanished without a trace over decades and centuries, spawning all sorts of theories as to what may have happened, some a bit more likely and some a bit crazy!

Though tales of mysterious activity happening in the area may date back centuries, a story from 1945 really kicked off the modern obsession with the Bermuda Triangle. Just after 2:00 p.m. on December 5, Flight 19, a group of five torpedo bombers, took off from a base in Fort Lauderdale,

Florida, for a two-hour training flight. The planes had more than a dozen crewmen on board, led by Lieutenant Charles Carroll Taylor. But two hours later, it became clear that something was wrong.

Radio messages from Taylor indicated that something wasn't right, and that the planes weren't where they were supposed to be, or even where they thought they were. Taylor's messages said things like, "Both my compasses are out—I'm over land. I'm sure I'm in the [Florida] Keys....I don't know how to get to Fort Lauderdale." These kinds of messages continued for two hours, and it seemed that the group somehow believed they had ended up in the Gulf of Mexico to the west, when they shouldn't have been anywhere near there, and were trying to get back to Florida.

At one point, Taylor announced that they were low on fuel and would have to "ditch" the planes in the water. Then the radio fell silent. A so-called "flying boat" was dispatched after dark to search for the planes and crew, but it seems to have exploded in the air and crashed. An exhaustive search of the area over the following several days found no trace of the Flight 19 planes, no wreckage, and no survivors. The five aircrafts and all the men had simply vanished.

Over the years, imaginative people have added to the story. There were reports of additional radio transmissions, where Taylor said, "Even the ocean doesn't look as it should," and "Don't come after me," but these have never been proven to exist. So what actually happened? Taylor's compasses seem to have malfunctioned, as he thought he was in a much different place than he was. But why did they malfunction, when they had been inspected shortly before the flight? And though Taylor was new to the area, he had a lot of flight experience; how would he have mistaken something like the Bahamas for the Florida Keys? And how did Flight 19 manage to wander around in the air for more than five hours without having a clue as to where they were?

The planes were assumed to have crashed at sea, but some tantalizing evidence indicates that at least one of them made it back to Florida and crashed near the Everglades. A plane discovered there in 1989 matched the description of Taylor's plane, and radar reportedly picked up other planes on the day the five went missing. Unfortunately, the plane has now vanished (either from vandalism or into the swamp), so a definitive identification is impossible. It may well be one of the missing planes from Flight 19, but again, how did they get so turned around? Was some mystery out in the Triangle responsible for their doom?

BEN PADILLA AND THE BOEING 727

In May 2003, an American aircraft mechanic and private pilot named Ben Padilla went to work on a job in Angola, in southwest Africa. His task was to fix up a privately owned Boeing 727. He and his assistant, John Mikel Mutantu, worked on the plane to get it back into shape to fly again. Padilla had done this kind of work all over the world, so nothing seemed unusual about this particular job. And for the most part, there wasn't. Padilla and Mutantu did the work required, and before long, the jet was in good condition again. On the evening of May 25, they were on board, checking out various things, when something unexpected happened, or at least, so it seemed to people outside the plane.

The 727 started up and began to taxi down the runway, meandering a bit. The air traffic controllers couldn't communicate with anyone on board, but there should have been only the two mechanics in there. The jet entered the runway without clearance, and without its lights or transponder on. It started down the runway and took off, heading southwest over the Atlantic Ocean, and has never been seen since.

There are a few important things to know about this situation. This kind of 727 takes three people to fly it, and in any case, Padilla only had a pilot's license for small aircraft, not for something this large. Mutantu couldn't fly at all. So how did this gigantic airplane even take off?

The answer is almost certainly that others were hiding out on the plane, and that they hijacked it and fled into the night. But if that's so, then where did they go?

Intelligence services were immediately worried that the plane might be used for a terrorist attack; the terrible events of 9/11 were fewer than two years in the past. But as days and weeks and months wore on without anything happening, this fear became less and less important.

Obviously, the jet was meant for some other use. But how does an airliner this big and the two men known to be aboard just disappear?

Many people think it crashed into the ocean, while others say that it may have been flown to a secret location elsewhere in Africa and then stripped for parts. Some people have suggested that the owners even set this whole thing up, because they were unhappy with the jet they had bought. If they could say it was hijacked or stolen, their insurance company might be forced to pay for it.

All of these situations are possible, but in the end, no one knows what happened to the 727, if anyone else was on board, and whether the two mechanics were involved or are still alive. It's one of the great mysteries of modern aviation.

GLENN MILLER

Glenn Miller was an American musician known for being a bandleader, big band trombonist, and composer in the swing era and was the best-selling recording artist from 1939 to 1942.

In 1942, Miller became determined to join the war efforts during World War II. However, due to Miller being thirty-eight years old, he was unable to be drafted. After the Navy declined his volunteer services, Miller wrote to the US Army and asked to work in the Army band. He played his last civilian concert on September 27, 1942, in Passaic, New Jersey, before joining the Allied Forces band.

He reported to Omaha, Nebraska, in October 1942 as a captain in the Army Specialist Corps before being transferred to the Army Air Forces. He played the trombone in Montgomery, Alabama service clubs, recreation halls, and on the radio, where he promoted civil service.

Miller helped to form a large marching band in an attempt to modernize military music and recorded Office of War Information propaganda in Abbey Road Studios to encourage the war effort. Eventually, he worked with actor David Niven in the radio service created by the BBC and Supreme Headquarters Allied Expeditionary Force (SHAEF), where his band's office was located. After a bomb landed near his office, he relocated to Bedford, England, and the day after he left England, his former office was bombed, killing seventy of his former coworkers.

On December 15, 1944, Miller was scheduled to fly from Bedford to Paris on a single-engine UC-64 Norseman. Miller, along with Lieutenant Colonel Norman Baessell and the pilot, John Morgan, disappeared over the English Channel. Miller was survived by his wife, Helen, and two children.

There are several theories regarding Miller's disappearance, with the most common explanation being that the plane flew into cold weather and suffered from carburetor icing, which would have caused the aircraft to lose power, and crash into the English Channel, and if Miller and the other passengers survived, they would have died from hypothermia within twenty minutes of hitting the water.

Some conspiracy theories include Miller being sent on a secret mission to negotiate a peace deal with the Nazi Party, where he was assassinated (Miller was not a solider in any way—he only played for the band); that he died from a heart attack in a Paris brothel; and that his aircraft was hit by Allied bombers by accident. A later investigation claimed that Miller had become impatient after his passenger flight was canceled due to poor weather conditions, but had enlisted Baessell without telling his chain of command.

MALAYSIA AIRLINES FLIGHT 370

On March 8, 2014, an international passenger flight operated by Malaysia Airlines disappeared while flying from Malaysia to Beijing. 227 passengers and twelve crew members vanished along with it.

The crew communicated with air traffic control (ATC) about thirty-eight minutes after takeoff, when the plane was over the South China Sea. It disappeared from ATC radar screens mere minutes later, but was tracked by military radar for another hour. This showed that it deviated from its original flight path, traveling westward across the Malay Peninsula and Andaman Sea. The next communication from the plane was a "log-on" request, after which the satellite data unit aboard the aircraft responded to hourly status requests which went unanswered by any crew members. The final status request that the aircraft acknowledged occurred an hour and forty minutes after the plane was scheduled to arrive in Beijing— seven hours after final contact was made by the crew. The plane left radar range 200 nautical miles northwest of Penang Island (in northwestern Peninsular Malaysia).

The resulting search for the missing airplane became the most expensive in aviation history, and lasted for three years before the agency heading the operation suspended its activities. In 2018, a separate private contractor launched another search, but it was ended after six months without progress. The lack of information was the source of much criticism, particularly from relatives of the passengers and the Chinese public (as most of the passengers were Chinese). Air transport industry safety recommendations and regulations have been updated in an attempt to prevent circumstances like that of Flight 370.

All 239 people who were on board are presumed dead.

There has been much speculation as to what may have happened to the plane. Many theories have been proposed and later rejected: among them, the idea that the plane was hijacked or that cargo was sabotaged. Two

men boarded the plane with stolen passports, so they were investigated for potential terrorist motives, but ultimately they were believed to be asylum seekers. The cargo included lithium ion batteries that could have ignited. US officials believe that the most likely explanation is that someone in the crew reprogrammed the autopilot, and it seems that Captain Zaharie, the pilot, was the prime suspect in this theory.

The two most widely believed theories are that the power was lost during flight and that at some point the crew became unresponsive, potentially as a result of hypoxia (oxygen deficiency due to low cabin pressure). The plane could have continued flying on autopilot until it disengaged, where the aircraft would have entered a spiral dive. Several pieces of the plane washed ashore in the western Indian Ocean in 2015 and 2016; one of these pieces—the flaperon—was analyzed, and showed that the landing flaps were not extended at the time of the crash, supporting this theory.

Other theories range from "the plane was consumed by a black hole" to "the plane was hit by a meteor" and "the plane was abducted by aliens." To this day, we have no concrete proof of what happened to the plane or its passengers.

CHAPTER 3
INTO THE WILD

THE WILDERNESS EVOKES a broad range of emotions in people. Perhaps you're someone who enjoys taking a walk in the woods, and finds being surrounded by nature relaxing. Perhaps you've visited a national park or traveled to see the wonders of the natural world and found yourself in awe of its majesty. Maybe you've gone camping, and spent a night or even days in the middle of nowhere, with no civilization in sight. Learning how to fend for ourselves in this environment is a common subject for children's groups/clubs, TV shows, books, videos, and so on. We've all seen books, TV shows, and movies where terrifying things happen in the woods, and we'd all like to think that we're more prepared than the people who never leave the forest, but we cannot know for certain. This chapter will tell the tales of those people—those who went out into the wild and never returned.

VANISHING ALONG VERMONT'S LONG TRAIL

The Long Trail is a wilderness path that runs from Vermont's border with Massachusetts to the border with Canada. Though popular with hikers and nature lovers, the years between 1945 and 1950 brought a strange series of unexplained disappearances that are still unsolved.

In 1945, an experienced hunter and guide, Middie Rivers, was leading a group through the area when he vanished after being separated from them. Rivers was in his seventies and knew the area very well, but a massive search for him over the following week turned up nothing.

In 1946, eighteen-year-old Paula Welden decided to go for a hike along the trail, taking a break from her college classes. She was last seen on December 1, and failed to turn up for school on Monday. Again, a wide-ranging search found no trace of her.

Exactly three years later, in 1949, a man in his sixties, James Telford, also vanished. Some accounts say he was on the trail, but others say he was even more mysteriously on a night bus and disappeared somewhere on the way to his destination to a town nearby.

In November 1950, Martha Jones disappeared in the same area. Some had thought she'd run off to be with her boyfriend in Virginia, but this turned out not to be the case. Like the others, she was never found.

Finally, just one month later, Frances Christman went out to visit a friend and apparently walked part of the trail to get there, only to disappear and never be seen again.

The most obvious answer to these cases was that a serial killer was lurking in the woods, waiting for victims. But the fact that none were ever found is very strange. Maybe the killer was getting bold and wanted to taunt the authorities in that case? But the choice of victims was all over the place in terms of age, gender, and so on, which is not a typical serial killer pattern.

The victims tended to disappear between November and January, and most were last seen in the late afternoon—but these are the only things that connect them.

The disappearances stopped after Christman went missing, but the area has long been known for unexplained phenomena, such as UFO sightings, Bigfoot-like creatures, ghostly forms in the woods, mysterious voices on the local radio, and more. A very human killer might have attacked the victims, but the lack of any trace is very strange indeed.

What happened to these poor people? Only the Long Trail and its wilderness know for sure.

MAUREEN KELLY

Maureen Kelly was a fairly typical nineteen-year-old, free of cares and worries, and looking to have fun. So when she had the chance to go on a camping trip with friends in Washington's Gifford Pinchot National Forest in June 2013, she jumped. Her friends remember her being excited about the trip, even if it was a bit of an impulsive decision to go. Things started off well; everyone had been camping before and knew what they were doing. But one evening, Maureen started acting a bit strangely.

She told her friends she wanted to go on a "spiritual quest" and headed into the woods by herself for a while. The others thought this seemed a bit weird, because they had never heard her mention anything like this before. A few of them thought she wasn't really behaving like herself. But nobody tried to stop her, and she promised she'd be back by midnight. She left them soon after, carrying a compass, a small knife, some matches, and a fanny pack, and she disappeared into the woods.

Her friends still weren't sure what to make of it, but by midnight she wasn't back, and they began to get worried. They called out for her, looked around, and heard and found nothing, so they called the sheriff and reported her missing. This was out of character for her: first to go off into the woods at night by herself, and second, to not be prepared. But it was about to get a lot stranger.

A search revealed that Maureen had removed her clothes, folded them up, and continued on her way. She was out on a chilly night, walking barefoot and wearing nothing. It made absolutely no sense, even as part of a spiritual quest. It was ridiculously dangerous and was completely unlike her. A search using dogs was actually able to pick up her trail, so for a short time, there was hope. But then, things got even weirder. Her trail led down a very steep ravine to a creek, and back up the other side, up to a dirt fire road (used by fire trucks to get into an area to help fight forest fires). And there, Maureen's trail stopped.

No one could figure out how someone wearing no clothes and walking barefoot in the dark could have made her way down into a ravine and back up the other side. It would have been difficult even for an experienced hiker, but the evidence says that's exactly what happened.

Her Facebook profile gave some clues: a few days before, she had posted about "spreading love" and being a "guru" (teacher), and a few friends said that she had mentioned a spiritual quest of some kind, but didn't give any details. The official explanation is that she injured herself in the dark, fell somewhere, and froze to death in the cold.

But no body or any trace of her has ever been found, and there is no explanation for how she managed to make a steep descent and climb in the dark. And why was there no sign of her after the fire road?

This private road was for firefighters' use only, so there wouldn't have been any cars up there.

These kinds of stories are strangely common: someone seems mysteriously drawn out into the wilderness, maybe acting out of character, and then is never seen again. The following story is another good example.

TERRENCE SHEMEL WOODS JR.

Woods was a talented young filmmaker who was especially good at producing documentaries. He had traveled the world and worked in some fairly remote outdoor places, so he was no stranger to tough shoots. In October 2018, Woods and a crew were out in the wilderness of Idaho, making a documentary about an old gold mine. On October 5, the crew had done a long day's work, and Woods was a bit quieter than usual. People assumed he was tired, something that could easily happen on one of these long shoots. But he was about to do something no one could ever explain.

As the crew was wrapping up and packing, Woods was near the edge of a cliff, when the production manager got a funny feeling and looked over to where Woods had been. He wasn't there. The production manager, fearing that maybe he had fallen off the cliff, got out of his vehicle and dashed over, only to see Woods running down the side. The production manager explained, "I've never seen anyone run that fast. At that point I yelled to the crew to get in a vehicle and go to the main road. I proceeded down the cliff...but he kept running. Due to my professional SAR [search and rescue] training, I stopped running after him out of fear he'd be further scared. So I went back topside...on the main road."

Woods just ran away into the forest, and that was the last anyone ever saw of him. Nobody could explain why he had acted like that, much less how he could have just disappeared without a trace. As with Maureen Kelly, it was as if something were calling to him, and he went to it, and it took him away. But unlike Kelly, who gently wandered into the night, Woods seemed to be in a big hurry to get away, almost like he was running from something, rather than to something.

Did an unseen power chase him? Did he see something the others didn't? If so, why did he run away from his friends, rather than to them?

A search team arrived, with dogs, but they were not able to find a scent or a trail to follow. Even weirder, there were no tracks in the fresh snow that had fallen. If he'd been running through the snow, he would have left footprints. Like in the Kelly case, he seemed to have gotten to a certain place and just vanished.

His family said that he seemed fine before going on the shoot, though a few said that perhaps he was a bit anxious about something. He did text his father to say that he was coming home early, though he didn't explain why. And the day that he ran off, he sent his dad some footage of a river in a canyon with no explanation. Did Woods throw himself into it? If so, a body was never found. Woods seemed to be fine and not have any mental health issues or be under any real stress, so why he suddenly bolted away into nothingness can't be explained. Did he run toward something in the wilderness?

Or was something after him?

SUSAN ADAMS

The vanishing of Susan Adams is less astonishing than that of Terrence Woods, but no less mysterious. Again, Adams seemed to leave a trail that suddenly stopped. Interestingly, Adams, who was an experienced camper, also disappeared in Idaho, near the state's border with Montana, just like Woods. Is something out there that is drawing people in?

This incident occurred in September 1990. Susan and her husband, Tom, were on an extended camping trip with a group of hunters, guides, and outdoorspeople, and for the first week, everything was fine. On September 29, Tom decided to go on an overnight hunting trip with some of the others, and Susan decided to stay behind. They parted, and all seemed well. At around 9:00 a.m. the following day, Susan decided to go bird-watching in a meadow close by. She told the camp cook about her plans and went off to see what kinds of birds she could spy in the area. And that was the last time anyone saw her.

By late afternoon, Tom and the others had returned, but Susan hadn't. So of course, they all set off on a search, starting with the meadow. There was nothing unusual there, but Tom noticed footprints—presumably Susan's—on a path leading out of the meadow.

But they stopped about twenty yards away. There was no sign of back-tracking, or of going off the path. Once again, it was as if Susan Adams, like Maureen Kelly and Terrence Woods, just evaporated.

There were no other clues and night was falling, so the group headed back to camp, hoping that Susan would make her way back from an extended hike. Unfortunately, she didn't turn up. The following morning, the campers contacted the police and rangers, and they conducted a big search covering several miles, but again, they couldn't find Susan, or any sign of her. After a week of searching and with snow starting to fall, they had to give up. Some theorized that she had gotten injured or been attacked by a wild animal, but there were no signs of any struggle, other than few more footprints that seemed older and could have belonged to anyone. Also, the meadow wasn't that far away from camp, so if she were attacked, someone would have heard her screaming for help. Her leaving the meadow seemed to be quite peaceful and voluntary. In any case, she was never found, and no real clues about what happened to her were ever found.

All three of these cases are weirdly similar. Someone goes out into the wilderness, almost as if drawn to it, and then they vanish. What's really happening? Given that Kelly's and Adams's tracks just stop, it does almost seem like something lifted them up and took them away. But what? Are these examples of UFO abductions? Bigfoot abductions? Or are there other ancient powers in some natural areas that don't like visitors and sometimes whisk travelers away to places unknown?

BARBARA BOLICK

Barbara Bolick's case is yet another disappearance in the outdoors, but it's even stranger than the previous three, if the witness is to be believed. What makes this one so interesting and creepy is that Barbara disappeared while on a hike with someone else. Like so many of these cases, she just seemed to blink out of existence.

On July 18, 2007, Barbara and her husband, Carl, were entertaining Carl's cousin and their friend Jim Ramaker, who were visiting them in Montana. Sometime around 8:30 a.m., Barbara told Carl that she was taking Ramaker for a walk up to a scenic overlook, about twenty miles from their home; she always took their visitors up there for the great view.

They would drive to the trailhead and hike from there, and they only intended to be gone a few hours. But this time, they weren't back by noon. The cousin was starting to get a bit worried, but Carl wasn't.

Barbara was very fit and was a skilled hiker. She also carried a gun in her backpack, in case she encountered wild animals or other trouble. But soon, Carl got a phone call from a park ranger, telling him that Barbara had been reported missing.

Carl and his cousin drove up to the park site and met up with Jim Ramaker. The story he told was unbelievable. Jim and Barbara had gone up to see the scenery and stayed for a half hour or so, and then started to walk back. At some point on the trail, Ramaker had stopped to take in the views. He turned around to enjoy the beautiful landscape, while Barbara waited only twenty or thirty feet away.

He said he did this for no more than a minute, but when he turned around again, Barbara was gone. Just gone. It wasn't a heavily wooded area, but he couldn't see her anywhere. He searched for her, then came back on his own to report her missing. Helicopters and sniffer dogs searched the area, but no trace of her was found. And to this day, she's still missing.

Obviously, some suspected that Ramaker had done something. Did he deliberately kill her? He had no criminal record, and the police never

considered him a suspect; he cooperated with them fully and offered to help with the investigation. Did he accidentally knock her off a cliff? If so, then why lie about it? He could just say she slipped and fell. And in any case, a body was never found. Did a mountain lion or bear attack her? If so, how could Ramaker have not heard it, if she was that close? Perhaps she wasn't as close as he thought. Maybe she wandered off a bit farther while he was looking at the area, and was attacked by a mountain lion; they can be quite sneaky and quiet.

Still, there were no signs of a struggle. Two other men were seen walking a dog in the area at the same time, but witnesses said they didn't act suspicious in any way. Did Barbara secretly plan to run away? Why do it out there? And leave behind her passport and other important belongings, as well as a dog and a cat she adored? And if she did, why has no one seen her since?

Like the other cases, it's as if the wilderness just swallowed up Barbara and left no clues behind.

DENNIS MARTIN

Dennis Martin was a happy seven-year-old, typical for his age, who loved playing with his friends. In 1969, he was with his family on a camping trip on the Appalachian Trail in the Great Smoky Mountains National Park (which sits in parts of both North Carolina and Tennessee). After a hike, the family was resting, and several kids were playing hide-and-seek. Dennis's father watched as his son hid in some bushes, and didn't think much about it. By 4:30 p.m., Dennis hadn't been found, so his dad, knowing where he'd gone, went to get him. Except he wasn't there.

Family and friends immediately started looking for him, and alerted park rangers, who were out searching by that evening. The search got more intense, with helicopter, military personnel, and even the FBI getting involved. But after several weeks, they had found nothing except one footprint that might have been Dennis's, and a report of a child-size skeleton that was never confirmed.

This might have been just another tragic disappearance, but there was something super creepy that, strangely, the rangers never really followed up on, probably because they didn't believe it. Dennis was already missing by 4:30 p.m. About an hour later, some eight miles away from where he disappeared, the Keys family was also camping, when they were startled by something terrifying. They heard a loud, awful scream from somewhere in the woods, something that didn't sound like any animal they'd heard before.

When they looked into it, they said they saw what looked like a "man in a bear suit" or a "wild man" darting behind trees, as if trying to avoid being seen. The press never reported what they said next: it looked like the creature had a child slung over its shoulder. Was this Dennis? Was he still alive? We don't know, but it seems too much of a coincidence not to look into. The FBI wasn't interested in this, but Dennis's father and a park ranger tried making the walk to the area and found that it could be done in an hour.

So many questions remain. Did something abduct Dennis? If so, what was it? Was it a Bigfoot or a related creature? Was it a human "wild man" hiding out in the forest, and not wanting to be seen?

Except for the unconfirmed report of a skeleton, no trace of Dennis was ever found. It's not typical for a Bigfoot to attack humans with the intention to kill, much less eat, but if this was a Bigfoot, maybe it was starving? Or maybe what the Keyses saw didn't have Dennis at all, and he just got lost in the woods. The case remains unsolved.

DOUGLAS LEGG

On July 10, 1971, eight-year-old Douglas Legg was out with his family at the Santanoni Preserve of the Adirondack Mountains in northern New York. It's a remote area, filled with forests and lakes. Douglas, or "Dougie" as he was called, went out with his uncle for a hike around the area. But a half mile or so away from where they were staying, his uncle noticed a lot of poison ivy around, and told the boy to go back to the lodge and change from shorts to longer pants for protection; no one wants the itch that poison ivy gives!

The boy headed back to the lodge, and his brother and cousin saw him only fifty yards away from it. Some friends playing by a nearby lake shouted out to him to come join them, and he answered that he'd take a shortcut to get there. No one ever saw him again.

When Dougie didn't return, his uncle became very concerned. The family called the police, and a search was conducted with nearly 1,000 volunteers over the following several days. A sniffer dog picked up a trail that led to a pond, but when it was drained, nothing was in it. After that, heavy rains fell and erased any chance for a bloodhound to pick up his scent again. They tried searching for six weeks, but the search was reluctantly called off after that. No trace of Dougie was ever found.

What makes this case so strange is that Dougie was on a well-defined path, and he made it back to the lodge. His brother and cousin even saw him approaching it. But somehow, he never got back to his uncle, even though the path was wide and clear. It's not like he was wandering in the wilderness and got lost. It's possible that he decided to do something else instead, after he put on his pants. Maybe he decided to go exploring, but it would be odd that he didn't tell anyone he had a change of plans.

Could the uncle have been a suspect? It's possible, but if he was trying to harm Dougie, why send him all the way back to his family and the lodge? Why insist he change into pants? The uncle was never suspected of any wrongdoing, and he was as upset as everyone else.

In the 1990s, a man came forward to tell authorities that he had found a small skull and parts of a skeleton in 1973. He and his friend hadn't reported it at the time, because they were on leave from the Navy, but not where they were supposed to be, and they didn't want to get in trouble. The man took investigators to the area, but they weren't able to find anything, so whatever answers the skull may have given are now lost.

Like so many of these tales, it seems that a little boy just vanished on a well-walked trail between the lodge and...somewhere?

MATTHEW WEAVER

Matthew Weaver was young and had a lot to look forward to. He'd just moved out of his parents' California home and into his own place. He'd gotten a good job with a power line company, and had dreams of traveling the world when he'd saved up some money. Unfortunately, fate intervened in a bizarre fashion, and now, no one can find him.

On August 9, 2018, Matthew told his father that he was going out with a friend. He picked her up later that evening, and they hung out until about 2:00 a.m. on August 10. After that, he drove out to a remote location in the Santa Monica Mountains. At about 5:45 a.m., he posted a picture of the sunrise and the area on Snapchat, then set off on a hiking trail. Several hours later, the woman he'd been out with received some mysterious text messages from him. They read: "Like some crazy is going onsh— is going on" and "I jusst to talk while I have the chance." She didn't know what they meant, but he sounded like he was in trouble or afraid. The spelling and bad grammar made it look like he sent them in a hurry, or was running from something.

Weaver's family immediately started to search for him, but they found nothing. The following day, things got even more unnerving. At about 1:30 a.m., some hikers and campers in the same area called 911 after

hearing what sounded like cries for help. A highway patrolman nearby also said that he'd heard shouting or screaming, and something that sounded like "He's got a gun!" Unfortunately, they weren't able to figure out what any of this was. Matthew's car was found, and the car keys had been dropped only about twenty-five feet down the trail. Drone footage also spotted a baseball cap and a T-shirt that might have been his, but no sign of him.

His friends later told the family that Weaver had hit his head a few days before he went missing. They worried that he might have suffered a concussion or other brain injury that would make him act strangely, but right up until the night he disappeared, they hadn't noticed anything unusual. It's possible that something came over him later and he became disoriented after going out for an early morning hike, but it seems like he should have been found by now. Also, what did those hikers hear a day later? Was it related to Weaver's disappearance? Did he get lost, and manage to stumble into some kind of drug deal or other crime being committed? Was he running from someone when he texted his friend? Did they find him, kill him, and bury the body somewhere in the wilderness?

Matthew's disappearance is oddly similar to others we've seen, where someone seems to be acting normal, but then feels "called" to a wild area, walks into it, and vanishes. What is it about these remote places that seems to draw people in, only for them never to be seen again?

MISSING PERSONS IN THE US NATIONAL PARKS

By now, we are pretty used to hearing about people going missing; often they are kidnappings or other crimes, and usually people are found, both alive and dead. But sometimes they're not, as you know from the mysteries in this chapter.

When researchers step back and look at the bigger picture of missing persons, they start to see patterns that are more than a little creepy.

There are some weirdly similar stories across time and place that make them seem possibly connected. In the national parks of the United States, for example, there seem to be a very large number of missing persons cases, with no good explanations. So what might be happening?

A former policeman and now paranormal investigator named David Paulides started researching the records of people who vanished without a trace in the national parks. He began his work after being approached by at least one park ranger who quietly expressed concerns that not enough was being done, and that the cases themselves were truly mysterious. Paulides and other researchers came to believe that at least 1,600 people have gone missing in the parks, which, given how large they are and how much time they've been open, may not seem like that many. But remember that these are people who have completely vanished. No traces were ever found, or if they were, strange circumstances often surrounded them, like the things we've already seen: people removing clothes and going into the wilderness, babies being moved impossible distances, people feeling almost like they've been "summoned" into the wilderness, and so on. These are odd, especially in this day and age, when anyone can be found pretty easily, using phones and satellites.

An even bigger mystery surrounds the parks. The estimate of 1,600 is just that: a guess. This is because, apparently, there are no official records about missing persons in the park system, at least none the public can view. Remember that this is public land—it belongs to all Americans—and yet we're told no data about possible crimes are collected in one place? It makes no sense.

Paulides and others think that the information is being hidden, because the Park Service is worried that if the true numbers and stories got out, people would stop visiting. He did more research and found about thirty "hot spots" for disappearances, most with twenty to thirty people having vanished in each place. Disappearances most often happened in late afternoon, and it was typical for the person just to vanish. Sometimes clothes are found, neatly folded up (like in the case on page 79), or, if a body is found, the clothing is often missing. In other weird cases, a body shows up somewhere that was already searched, often much later. There's no way it would have been missed before. It's like rescue teams are being deliberately taunted. Now, if this had only happened once or twice, it could be ignored. But when these things happen over and over, we have to wonder and even worry about what might be happening.

Certainly, some people just get lost, and, horribly, some people are kidnapped and killed. But a lot of these disappearances are just plain weird, creepy, and unexplainable. Are these vanishings evidence of mass alien abduction? Or are there forces in the wilderness that we don't yet know about? Forces that don't want us to be there?

JOEY AND BILLY HOAG

Joey and Billy Hoag, ages thirteen and eleven, were in trouble. But it was the kind of trouble that kids their age usually get into. It was May 1967 in Hannibal, Missouri, and the Hoag boys had been out exploring a cave and came home covered in mud and dirt. Their parents weren't happy with them, and punished them by telling them that they weren't allowed to go farther than the front yard the following day. Boys being boys, they didn't listen, and snuck out to do more exploring on May 10. And that was the last time anyone ever heard from them.

As their parents searched for them, they learned from a neighbor that, sure enough, the boys had gone back to explore the caverns of Murphy's Cave. The neighbor had even seen them going in, not knowing they were grounded for the day. The boys' sister later recalled that they had explored and mapped out parts of it, and loved going there. Only this time, they didn't come back. At the same time, another boy named Craig Dowell also went missing, but no one was sure whether or not he had joined the Hoag boys. The fact that they were all missing at the same time suggests that he probably did.

The caves and surrounding areas were searched, but no trace of any of them was found, and never would be. Years went by, and the stress on the family was terrible, but no clues emerged as to what might have happened. The police department issued a statement warning young people to stay out of the caves by themselves, even if they thought they knew them, because there was always a chance they could get hurt—or worse.

That was good advice, of course, but it didn't answer the question: Where did the missing boys go? If they'd been injured or even killed, they would have been found eventually, but again, they were just gone, as if they'd never been there. It makes you wonder what they found in those caverns... or maybe, what found them.

AMY WROE BECHTEL

Amy Wroe Bechtel was an American woman who went missing while jogging in 1997. Originally from California, Bechtel graduated from the University of Wyoming and married rock climber Steve Bechtel. Amy Bechtel was planning on trying out for the 2000 Summer Olympics for competitive long-distance running. She and her husband lived in Lander, Wyoming, at the time of her disappearance.

On July 24, 1997, Bechtel told Steve that she had to run some errands around town and go to the Wind River Fitness Center to teach a class for children about weight lifting. After teaching her class, Bechtel went to Camera Connection near her home at approximately 2:30 p.m. Bechtel then stopped at Gallery 332 and spoke to the proprietor, Greg Wagner. Wagner told police that she continuously glanced at her watch and seemed hurried; this was the last known sighting of Bechtel. Authorities believe that Bechtel then drove to Shoshone National Forest in order to practice the route of an upcoming race she had signed up for; several witnesses claim they saw a woman matching Bechtel's description running by the road. Steve returned home at around 4:30 p.m. and noticed his wife had not returned home. At 10:30 p.m., Steve reported his wife missing to police.

At 1:00 a.m. the next morning, Bechtel's car was discovered at a turnout at nearby Burnt Gulch. Within a few hours of Bechtel being reported missing, authorities, Steve, and Bechtel's friends and family began an extensive search. Over the next few days, police searched several nearby lakes and mines, but with no evidence. Police initially believed Bechtel had been attacked by a bear or mountain lion, or fallen victim to the elements. By August, police began to focus their investigation on Bechtel's husband, after finding a journal where Steve described violence toward his wife and even included a poem that described murdering someone. Steve later claimed the journal contained song lyrics for his band. Amy's brother, Nel Wroe, also told police that he had seen Amy with a bruise. She had brushed it off, but Nel claimed she had not been able to meet his eyes. Steve did not cooperate with police, but did have an alibi that was confirmed by his friends, who told authorities that they had been rock climbing at the time of Bechtel's disappearance. However, Steve refused to take a polygraph test. A witness also told police she had seen a truck similar to Steve's in the area where Bechtel disappeared.

In 2003, a hiker found a watch that was similar to one that Bechtel owned, but it was unconfirmed that it belonged to her.

Another suspect that was considered was Dale Wayne Eaton, also known as the Great Basin Killer, who murdered Lisa Marie Kimmell in 1988. Eaton's brother told police that he often camped near Burnt Gulch around the time of Bechtel's disappearance, but police were never able to confirm his whereabouts, and Eaton refused to talk to police.

In 2004, Amy Bechtel was declared legally dead at the behest of Steve, and he remarried later that year.

CHRISTINA CALAYCA

Christina Calayca was a twenty-year-old Filipino-Canadian woman from Toronto who went missing in 2007. Coincidentally, at the same time that Calayca disappeared, her cat, Oreo, also disappeared and never returned. Prior to her disappearance, Calayca had been a part of a hiking group that got lost on Seaton Hiking Trail, but found her way out after wandering around the forest.

During the 2007 Civic Holiday weekend, Calayca traveled with her cousin, Faith Castulo, and two friends from Youth for Christ, Eddy Migue and J. B. Benedict, to Rainbow Falls Provincial Park in Ontario, where Calayca held a leadership position. All four were experienced campers and told work colleagues where they were going, but Calayca's mother did not know their exact location. The group arrived at the campsite on August 5 and set up camp. After midnight, the last photo of Calayca was taken. At around 6:30 a.m., Calayca asked Migue to come with her to the comfort station, and the pair decided to jog back to the camp; on their jog back, the pair split up. Calayca went toward Rainbow Falls and was never seen again. Migue returned to the campsite, and the rest of the group woke up around 9:30 a.m. The group did not initially worry about Calayca being missing, as they thought she was taking a walk in the woods. At 11:00 a.m., the group began to search for Calayca around the park but were unable to locate her. They left a note at the camp for her in case she returned. At 2:00 p.m., the group officially reported Calayca missing to the Ontario Provincial Police after informing park staff.

Searches were conducted for at least seventeen days and covered all fifty-three kilometers of the Casque Isles Trails, and were supplemented by marine and aerial searches. Authorities used a standard lost hiker profile to try to find Calayca but found nothing officially linked to her. Calayca's mother also paid for several private searches.

As of 2022, Sgt. Don Webster with the Ontario Provincial Police told the media that the investigation is still active, and police have some information that has not been made public. Calayca's whereabouts are currently unknown, but there are several theories, including Calayca being

attacked by a bear or getting lost, which experts have found to be unlikely. Calayca's strong relationship with her family has led investigators to rule out Calayca intentionally disappearing. Calayca's family and internet sleuths believe that Calayca was a victim of foul play.

Some believe she could have been mistaken for an Indigenous woman and killed by someone who targets Indigenous women, similar to the nearby "Highway of Tears," where there have been several cases of murdered and missing Indigenous women. Others wonder if she was victimized by a police officer engaging in the phenomenon of "starlight tours," an occurrence where police officers have been known to kidnap Indigenous people and leave them in wilderness areas.

CHAPTER 4

INTO THE DEPTHS

THERE ARE HUNDREDS OF THOUSANDS of people with a fear of the ocean. And it's not hard to understand why—while water covers about 70% of our Earth, more than 80% of it remains unexplored. What lurks in the depths that we have yet to witness, have yet to name? Beyond the creatures and forces that could be waiting just beneath the surface, the power of the water itself is something to behold. From mighty, rushing whitewater rivers to freezing Arctic seas to massive tidal waves, water is an untamed element that you wouldn't wish to encounter without proper preparation. Even with all the preparation in the world, the nature of water is such that we can never be truly certain what it will bring. This chapter tells the stories of those who were claimed by the depths, or the creatures or forces therein, and never resurfaced.

THE MARY CELESTE

The case of the *Mary Celeste* is one of the classic vanishings in nautical history. On December 5, 1872, a ship called the *Dei Gratia* was sailing from New York to southern Spain, and encountered another ship on the ocean. It had masts and seemed to be adrift, or else was being sailed very badly. The captain and some other crew decided to investigate, and got in a smaller boat to row to this mystery. They could see the name of the ship—*Mary Celeste*—painted clearly on the stern.

Intrigued and maybe a little spooked, they went aboard. No crew came out to meet them. In fact, they searched up and down and found no one at all on board. The ship was abandoned. Now, if the ship were in bad shape, damaged, taking on water and sinking, and so on, one might expect that it could have been abandoned, but the really curious thing was that the ship was in perfect condition. Its cargo, plenty of food, the sails were all fine. The crew simply had no reason to leave the ship behind. Even weirder, all the crew's personal items and clothing were still there, which means they didn't just pack up and leave. In the captain's cabin were breakfast dishes, some still with porridge and half-eaten eggs. The people on board must have disappeared recently, because the food hadn't molded or spoiled.

The entire crew seemed to have decided to abandon ship and leave everything behind right in the middle of the ocean. The sails seemed to have been set freshly, so it couldn't have been drifting for a long time, even though the last ship's log entry had been on November 24, eleven days earlier. Even the lifeboat was still in place, so the crew couldn't have left that way. It was like they all just decided to jump into the ocean at once. It made absolutely no sense.

And to this day, it still doesn't. There have been many explanations over the years. The "official" explanation was that the crew got into some of the alcohol cargo, killed the captain, and then left on another boat, but this doesn't seem likely. They wouldn't have left everything behind.

A few clues were disturbing. There seemed to be bloodstains near a deck rail, next to what looked like a cut in the wood made by an ax, but not

everyone thought that's what it was. Also, the ship's chronometer (a kind of clock for marine navigation), another measuring tool, and some cargo papers were missing. But this was hardly anything to go on, and didn't explain the mystery.

In 1913, an account by a man named Abel Fosdyk claimed that he had been aboard the ship, and that a special deck had been built for the captain's daughter. One day, the captain and a crew member were talking about how best to swim, and one jumped into the water to show how it could be done in full clothing; the rest of the crew gathered on the deck to watch. It collapsed, sending them all into the ocean, where a school of sharks soon finished them off. Fosdyk somehow survived and drifted to the coast of Africa. The problem is, there is no record of this anywhere else, and Fosdyk got several details about the ship wrong. So it seems this was a made-up story after all.

No one knows what really happened to the *Mary Celeste*, besides that its entire crew vanished without a trace and left everything behind.

THE SARAH JOE

The case of the *Sarah Joe*, a small boat lost off the coast of Hawaii, is one of the more mysterious lost-at-sea tales of the past several decades. At first, it seemed like just a tragic accident: five friends took a boat out for some sailing off the coast of Maui, only to encounter a bad storm and go missing. But ten years later, things got weird.

On the morning of February 11, 1979, five friends took the *Sarah Joe* out for a cruise. It was a small motor-powered vessel, only seventeen feet long, and nothing special. The friends were looking forward to a few hours out on a beautiful day. But before long, a storm moved in, and not just any storm—a very violent one with gale-force winds and water swells of up to forty feet. It became obvious that this could be deadly to anyone in a small boat, and although several other boats made it back to shore, the *Sarah Joe* did not.

The following day, the Coast Guard launched a search, covering more than 70,000 square miles of surrounding ocean over five days, as well as looking at some of the small nearby islands, in case the five had managed to make it to one of them. Unfortunately, they found nothing, and everyone was forced to conclude that the boat and its five passengers had been lost at sea. That assumption held for ten years, but then something amazing happened.

Some of the original searchers were on a mission to study wildlife at the Marshall Islands and the Taongi Atoll, about 2,200 miles south and west of Hawaii, in the middle of the Pacific Ocean. These uninhabited little islands are home to trees and animals...and something far more interesting. A biologist named John Naughton discovered the remains of a fiberglass boat on the beach. It had a registration number on the side, and he was able to contact sources back in Hawaii to run it. It turned out to be the *Sarah Joe*! Somehow, that little boat had survived the storm and, probably by accident, floated more than 2,000 miles to land on this beach. That part of the mystery was solved.

But something even odder was about to unfold.

Nothing in the boat showed what might have happened, but about 100 yards away was a grave. It was a mound covered with coral and small stones; a bone was sticking out from it. As the researchers examined the grave, they found a skeleton, with a stack of papers on top, though nothing was written on them, and with pieces of tinfoil between them. This was bizarre. They didn't find any other graves or remains on the atoll, but they took one bone to be examined by a forensic team, leaving the rest out of respect.

Scientists were able to determine that the bone belonged to Scott Moorman, one of the five friends who'd sailed on that fateful day.

But because no one else was around, who had buried him?

One theory is that he died on the boat and drifted to the atoll, where some Chinese fishermen may have found the body and buried it; the papers on top with foil are a sign of a traditional Chinese burial practice. They may have done this out of respect, and left the body there. Perhaps the others were lost in the storm, and Scott survived for a while as his boat drifted without a motor, which would have taken at least three months to reach the atoll. But there's one more mystery to all of this. Four years before the discovery of the grave, another team had been to the islands—and they did not report anything unusual. Did the *Sarah Joe* drift for six or more years before landing on the island? If not, why was the grave never spotted?

BESSIE AND GLEN HYDE

The Hydes were newlyweds and ambitious. It was 1928, adventurers like Amelia Earhart were making names for themselves, and the Hydes wanted in on the excitement. They wanted to do something spectacular that they could write a book about and then go on a tour and make money off of. They married in April of that year, and soon after, they decided that their great adventure would be to raft down the Colorado River, through the entire Grand Canyon. If she succeeded, Bessie would be the first woman to do it, and that would surely bring her some fame and fortune! But their search for recognition seems to have been their downfall. And, certainly, a desire for fame was the wrong reason to try a dangerous trip like rafting the Colorado River!

They began their trip in Utah in October, and for the first week or two, things seemed to be going quite well. Glen wrote to his father that it had all been "great sport" so far. But by November, the river was getting more challenging, and the couple seemed to not be getting along so well. Maybe it wasn't turning out to be the fun adventure they thought it would be! They made it to an area called Bright Angel Creek, where they hiked up the canyon and got more supplies, and also asked a local photographer to take some pictures of them. They met up with Adolph Gilbert Sutro, an adventurer who wanted to join them for a short part of their journey.

A few days later, they dropped him off at a location called Hermit Camp, where he took some photos of them. In these pictures, the Hydes look

unhappy and exhausted. Maybe this was a clue about what would happen next? In any case, Sutro was the last person to see the pair. By the first week of December, they had not checked in or been seen, and Glen's dad called for a search and rescue mission.

Their boat was soon found. It was upright, and had their supplies and Bessie's journal; the last entry was dated November 30. But there was no sign of them, and they were never found. You might think that they simply fell into the river and drowned, but if so, it's odd that the boat didn't capsize, or take on water or any other damage, if it had just drifted down the river with no one to steer it. And would both have fallen in at the same time? Or maybe one fell in, and then the other did, trying to help?

But there were other theories. They had seemed to be arguing quite a lot, probably because the trip had turned out to be a dangerous and at times boring slog, not at all the adventure they'd hoped it would be. Some suspected that one may have struck and killed the other in anger, and then dumped the body overboard and fled, leaving the boat behind. But would Bessie have left her journal if this were the case? Or would Glen have left it, because she'd possibly written something bad about him?

Perhaps a third person killed both of them when they were camped on the riverside. But then, why not take all of the supplies from their boat? We'll never know, because they vanished. The Hydes did become famous, just not in the way they had hoped.

AIMÉE DU BUC DE RIVÉRY

Aimée du Buc de Rivéry was a French heiress who went missing in 1788. Aimée was born in December 1768 to French plantation owner Henri du Buc de Rivéry and Marie Anne Arbousset-Beaufond in the Caribbean island of Martinique.

While returning home from convent school in France, Aimée was lost at sea in July or August 1788, which has sparked many theories about what happened to her.

The most famous legend is that her ship was attacked and taken by Barbary pirates, whereupon she became a victim of the Barbary slave trade and was given as a gift to the Ottoman Sultan by the Bey of Algiers in Constantinople. According to this theory, Aimée became his wife and took the name Nakşîdil, and she allegedly introduced French ideas to the sultan and the Ottoman people. Some believe that her influence led to the death of the sultan by the Janissaries and the Ulema, the teaching of French to Abdul Hamid I, the inception of the first ambassador sent to Paris, the popularity of rococo style, and the encouragement of Selim III to start a French newspaper.

According to legend, Aimée influenced politics to the point that the Ottomans conceded their war with Russia and sided with England due to Napoleon divorcing her cousin-in-law, Joséphine. It is also thought that Aimée accepted Islam but remained Roman Catholic at heart and requested that a priest perform the last rites upon her death. According to this theory, Aimée had a son who became the sultan, and her tomb lies near the Hagia Sophia in what is now Istanbul, Turkey.

Although this legend has been popularized over the years, researchers and historians believe that Nakşîdil Sultan was ethnically Georgian, and the timeline of their lives disproves that they were the same person. Many historians believe that this legend was created with political motivations in order to justify the French and Ottoman alliance.

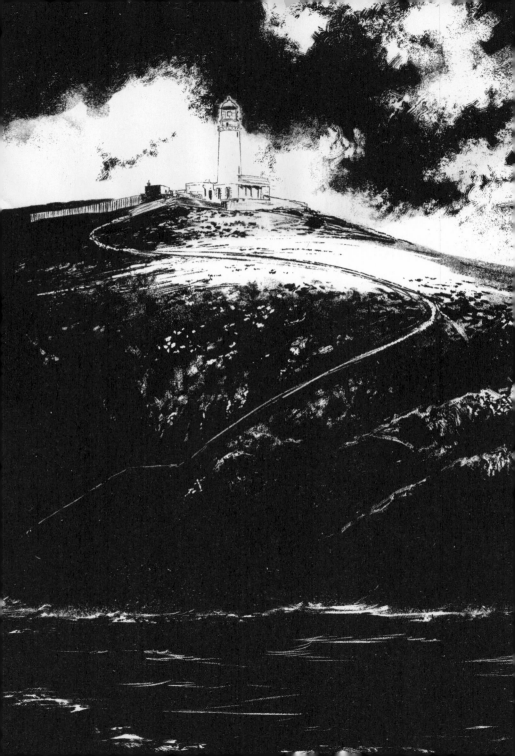

THE ABANDONED LIGHTHOUSE
AT EILEAN MOR

On December 26, 1900, a ship sailed out to the Flannan Isles, a group of very remote islands off the northwest coast of Scotland, uninhabited except for wildlife and a lighthouse on the island of Eilean Mor. Irish monks had once used these islands for sheep grazing, but it was said they wouldn't stay overnight on them, because they feared the spirits there. In any case, the ship's captain, James Harvey, wasn't concerned; he was bringing a new keeper, Joseph Moore, to the lighthouse, which was essential for guiding ships through that part of the ocean.

As they approached the island, lighthouse in sight, Harvey gave the order to blow the ship's horn. No one responded to it. This was unusual, because although there were only a few people at the lighthouse, someone was always on the lookout for ships. Moore rowed ashore, and walked up the steep flight of stairs that led to the lighthouse. Something felt wrong, very wrong. Moore made it to the lighthouse and had a look around. There should have been three lighthouse keepers, but no one was there. He found that two of the oilskin coats they used for going outside in the wind and rain were missing, but one was still hanging up. Also, there was half-eaten food on the table and a chair knocked over. It seemed like they had gotten up in a hurry and rushed outside, but why? The regulations stated that one man always had to be in the lighthouse. This would explain why one coat was left, but where was the one man? Another strange fact: the clock in the kitchen had stopped.

Official investigators arrived a few days later, but they were just as mystified. There was no sign of any of the keepers on the island or washed up on the shore at the bottom of the cliffs. They did find some ropes down at the landing platform, and the thought was that maybe these had fallen out of the crate that held them, and the keepers rushed down to try to grab them before they washed away, and the men were swept into the sea. But again, why would one go out without his coat? And if he stayed behind, where was he now?

The mystery only grew deeper when investigators read the log entries. An entry from December 12 reported severe winds unlike any they had ever seen, and one of the men was crying. Why? All were experienced and wouldn't have been upset by the wind. An entry for December 13 says that a storm was raging, but records show no storm in the area at that time. People from the nearby Isle of Lewis noted that they could see Eilean Mor. Further, the log said they were praying for the storm to stop. Even if there had been a storm, why would they have been afraid? The lighthouse was well built at the top of very sturdy rock cliffs, and they were in no danger.

Some speculate that the men argued and that one killed the other two before killing himself. It's possible, of course, but there isn't much evidence for it, beyond the fact that all three went missing.

Some believe the log entries are not real, and were added later. But even if they were, nothing explains how three experienced lighthouse keepers vanished during good weather.

Over the decades since, there have been stories about other lighthouse keepers hearing mysterious voices on the wind, sometimes whispering the names of the three lost keepers. Did something take them? Are they trapped in a ghostly dimension and still trying to escape? The true answers to their disappearance seem to have vanished along with them.

JOSHUA SLOCUM

Joshua Slocum was a Canadian-American who became the first person to sail around the world alone. Raised in Nova Scotia, Canada, Slocum became a seaman on a British merchant ship at age sixteen, and when he was eighteen, he passed the Board of Trade examination and became a qualified Second Mate. He quickly became a Chief Mate and settled in San Francisco, California. In 1887, Slocum, his second wife, and their children were shipwrecked in Brazil; Slocum built a boat from scratch and sailed them back to the United States. In 1895, Slocum set sail on an oyster boat called *Spray* to complete the first solo circumnavigation of the Earth and returned in June 1898. In 1899, he published his account of the voyage, *Sailing Alone Around the World*, where he described the storms, pirates, and illnesses that he experienced during his three years at sea. He met with President Theodore Roosevelt and his family and sailed with Archie Roosevelt on the *Spray*. By 1909, Slocum's finances were running low and he was planning on selling his farm on Martha's Vineyard.

On November 14, 1909, Slocum left Vineyard Haven, Massachusetts, in the *Spray* to go to the West Indies. He had also stated that he was planning on exploring the Orinoco River, Rio Negro, and Amazon River. At this point, Slocum was believed to be in poor health, and the *Spray* was decrepit and falling apart. Slocum and the *Spray* were never seen again. In 1910, his wife reported to the media that she believed he had been lost at sea. Due to the fact that Slocum had never learned to swim, some believe he drowned. Slocum was declared dead in 1924.

One theory regarding his disappearance was that he left deliberately because he was unhappy in his second marriage, due to his wife's dislike of sailing. It has also been theorized that Slocum was just another victim of the mysterious Bermuda Triangle, as some reports state he was planning to get supplies in Miami, Florida.

BEN MCDANIEL

Ben McDaniel is an American man who went missing while scuba diving in 2010. Originally from Tennessee, McDaniel went to stay in his family's beach house at Santa Rosa Beach in the Florida Panhandle after a series of financial and personal setbacks that included being in debt to the IRS, grieving his younger brother, Paul, who died from a stroke, and getting divorced. McDaniel's parents offered to support him financially while he took a break in Florida.

While in Florida, he began scuba diving, a hobby he'd enjoyed since he was fifteen. Despite being on the beach, McDaniel often went to Vortex Spring near Ponce de Leon to dive in freshwater. For experienced divers, Vortex Spring offers a cave with a depth of 115 feet. In order to go to the cave, a diver has to provide a cave diving certificate. Employees at Vortex Spring noted that McDaniel was a regular with a lot of diving knowledge and proper equipment; however, some said he was overconfident in his diving abilities. McDaniel's father told the media that no one at Vortex Spring wanted to be his diving partner, so he would do his dives alone.

In mid-August 2010, McDaniel went to visit his family and girlfriend in Tennessee, where he said he was researching cave diving in hopes of getting certified. McDaniel returned to Florida on the weekend of August 14, and his family never saw him again.

On August 18, McDaniel went to Vortex Spring again, where witnesses said that he was looking closely at the cave's entrance and spent most of his afternoon testing his equipment and writing in a dive log around the spring. At approximately 7:30 p.m., McDaniel went in for another dive after speaking to his mother on the phone. Two employees opened the gate into the cave and left the premises before seeing McDaniel decompress and return to the surface. McDaniel's truck was still in the parking lot the next two mornings, but this wasn't registered as strange.

After not seeing him for a few days, an employee of Vortex Spring called the Holmes County Sheriff's Office. Authorities sealed off the spring and found no indication of foul play. McDaniel's wallet (including over a thousand dollars in cash) and cell phone were found in his trunk, but his tanks, wetsuit, and other equipment were not found at the scene. Cadaver dogs supported the initial theory that McDaniel drowned while trying to escape the cave, but dive teams were unable to locate his body, though they found a few tanks that are believed to have belonged to McDaniel. However, they had the incorrect type of air.

Edd Sorenson, a recovery specialist with experience in cave diving, was unable to locate McDaniel and stated that there was no possible way that McDaniel could have gotten through some of the narrower passages, and there was no physical evidence that he had tried. After several divers searched the cave with no sign of McDaniel, police began searching the woods around Vortex Spring and swamps along the Vortex's outflow, to no avail.

The McDaniel family offered a large reward to divers that could go to deeper parts of the cave but rescinded it after a diver died attempting to go past the restrictions. It is unknown what McDaniel's fate was, but McDaniel's family believes he was murdered or someone covered up an accident. Some believe he staged the disappearance to avoid his financial troubles.

BAS JAN ADER

Bastiaan Johan Christiaan Ader, better known as Bas Jan Ader, was a Dutch artist and photographer who went missing in 1975. Ader grew up in a small village in the Netherlands. His father was executed by the Nazi Party two years after his birth for helping Jewish citizens escape the Holocaust. Ader took classes at the Gerrit Rietveld Academy in Amsterdam and graduated from the Otis College of Art and Design in Los Angeles, California, and later the Claremont Graduate University in Claremont, California. Ader taught at various colleges in Southern California and created many photographic and video works. One of his most famous art pieces, *I'm too sad to tell you,* is comprised of a three-minute silent film of him crying, his photographs, and a postcard written to friends.

On July 9, 1975, Ader left Cape Cod, Massachusetts, on a pocket cruiser boat named *Ocean Wave* to make a single-handed crossing of the North Atlantic Ocean. The trip was meant to be a part of a triptych he began in 1973 with a photo series of a lonely figure searching Los Angeles in the night. Ader believed he would finish the trip in two and a half months.

His empty boat was found nine months later on April 18, 1976, approximately 200 nautical miles due west of Land's End and 100 nautical miles southwest of Ireland. A fisherman took the *Ocean Wave* to A Coruña in Spain, but it was stolen sometime in May or June 1976. It is unknown how Ader died, and sightings of him and the *Ocean Wave* off the American East Coast and the Azores are not confirmed. Ader was an experienced sailor, having sailed a yacht from Morocco to California in 1962 and 1963, and his brother, Erik, also an experienced ocean sailor, believes Ader most likely fell overboard in heavy weather, due to interviews with witnesses in Spain who saw the *Ocean Wave* before it was stolen.

HENRY HUDSON

Henry Hudson was an English sea explorer during the early 17th century. Hudson was known for his exploration of northeastern North America and his search for the Northeast and Northwest Passages sea routes. Hudson sailed on several expeditions for the Muscovy Company, Dutch East India Company, Virginia Company, and British East India Company, where he was asked to find new passages for trade to commence. One of Hudson's voyages helped establish Dutch claims to Manhattan Island and the fur trade.

In 1610, Hudson captained a new ship, the *Discovery*, trying to find the Northwest Passage to Asia. After months mapping and exploring the eastern shores of what is now Hudson Bay in Canada, Hudson and his crew were forced to move ashore when the *Discovery* became trapped in ice in James Bay. When the ice finally cleared in the spring of 1611, Hudson wanted to continue to explore the Bay in hopes of finding the Passage, while the majority of his crew wanted to return home after spending the winter stuck in the Bay.

According to journals by survivor Abacuk Pricket, crew members Henry Greene and Robert Juet organized a mutiny against Hudson. According to Pricket, the mutineering crew members left Hudson, his son, sick crew members, and those loyal to Hudson on an open shallop boat, marooning them in Hudson Bay. Pricket's journal states the mutineers gave Hudson and his castaways clothing, pikes, an iron pot, some food, gunpowder, and other miscellaneous items. Hudson's boat tried to keep pace with the *Discovery*, but soon the ship left the castaways behind, never to be seen again. Sea navigators Thomas Button and Zachariah Gilliam conducted searches in the

area for Hudson and the others but found no trace of them. Pricket's journal has been heavily criticized for its potential bias. Both Greene and Juet did not survive the voyage back to England, and some believe Pricket blamed the mutiny on them in order to avoid piracy charges against him and the rest of the crew.

Only eight out of thirteen mutineers survived, and some were arrested in England and stood trial, but no punishment was given to the mutinous crew members. Several topographical features are named after Hudson, including the Hudson River in New York and New Jersey.

BISON DELE

Bison Dele, born Brian Carson Williams, was an American basketball player who disappeared in 2002. Dele began his collegiate basketball career at the University of Maryland before transferring to the University of Arizona. In 1991, Dele was drafted by the Orlando Magic and later played for the Los Angeles Clippers, Chicago Bulls, and Detroit Pistons. In 1998, he changed his name to Bison Dele in honor of his Native American and African ancestry. At the beginning of the 1999–2000 season, Dele retired from the NBA at the age of thirty. At the time of his retirement, he was the highest-paid player on the Pistons but decided to retire due to his poor relationship with the organization. After his retirement, Dele traveled to Lebanon, the Mediterranean, and Australia, eventually buying a catamaran and learning how to sail.

On July 6, 2002, Dele; his girlfriend, Serena Karlan; skipper Bertrand Saldo; and his brother, Miles Dabord, sailed from Tahiti on Dele's boat, the *Hakuna Matata*. No one but Dabord was seen or heard from again after the voyage, when he returned alone to Tahiti on July 20. Dele's family, the FBI, and police believed that Dele, Karlan, and Saldo were murdered by Dabord.

Investigators and Dele's family organized a sting operation to detain Dabord in Phoenix, Arizona, on September 6, 2002, after he forged Dele's signature

and used his passport to buy $152,000 worth of gold in Dele's name. Mexican police found that Dabord had been staying in a hotel in Tijuana. Around that time, the *Hakuna Matata*, which was registered under a different name, was found off the coast of Tahiti with its plates removed and possible bullet holes that had been patched up. Dabord also called his mother, claiming he would never hurt Dele and would not be able to survive in prison.

In 2002, Dabord purposely overdosed on insulin, slipping into a coma, and died in a California hospital. According to Dabord's account before his death, he stated that Karlan had been killed accidently while he and Dele were fighting, and Dele killed Saldo when he wanted to report her death, and Dabord killed Dele in self-defense.

HAROLD HOLT

Harold Holt was an Australian politician in the Liberal Party who served as the seventeenth prime minister of Australia from 1966 until his disappearance and presumed death in 1967. Holt was born in Sydney and raised in Melbourne, eventually studying law at the University of Melbourne. Holt was elected to the House of Representatives in 1935, made minister without portfolio in 1939, served in the Australian Army from 1939 to 1940, worked as Minister for Immigration from 1949 to 1956, was Minister for Labour and National Service from 1949 to 1958, and was sworn in as prime minister on January 16, 1966.

When Holt took office, he refused a security detail because he believed it was unnecessary. However, after a sniper shattered a window in his office and the leader of the opposition survived an assassination attempt, Holt accepted one bodyguard during work, but refused one while on holiday. According to his widow, Zara, the reason he refused protection while on holiday was to hide his extramarital affairs. Holt had a love for the ocean, particularly spearfishing, skin diving, and snorkeling. He had beach houses in both Portsea, Victoria, and Bingil Bay, Queensland. While he could tread water and hold his breath for long periods of time, Holt was not great at swimming on the surface. On two occasions, Holt had trouble breathing while he was snorkeling, one time even turning purple and vomiting. While having good health throughout his life, shortly before his disappearance his doctor advised him to be careful not to overdo it and avoid swimming and tennis for long periods of time.

Holt drove to Portsea on December 15, 1967, where he spent the weekend visiting family and friends, playing tennis, and hosting a dinner party. His wife stayed in Canberra to finish preparing for the upcoming annual Christmas party. On December 17, Holt woke up early, spoke to his wife on the phone, and bought insect repellent, peanuts, and newspapers at a local general store. That morning, the headline of *The Australian* read, "PM advised to swim less," and discussed his doctor's visit. It is unknown if Holt bought or read that paper. At 11:15 a.m., Holt and a group of four went to Point Nepean, but they left early, as it was a hot day. Holt and his friends went to Cheviot Beach to swim around 12:15 p.m. Only Holt and his friend Alan Stewart went into the water, because the others thought it was unsafe due to a large swell and rough currents. Stewart stayed close to the shore and felt a heavy undertow. Holt swam farther away from the shore and was dragged out to sea. Soon, he slipped under the waves, and his friends could no longer see him.

Victoria Police were contacted, and a major search of the area to try to find his body began around 1:30 p.m. Amateur divers, police divers, helicopters, watercraft, and two naval diving teams searched the water but made little progress, as there was limited equipment available and the conditions of the ocean were difficult. Authorities and divers continued to search the area, but poor weather and strong tides prevented them from finding any sign of Holt. The search was called off on January 5, 1968.

It is widely believed that Holt drowned, either overestimating his swimming abilities in such rough conditions, suffering a heart attack, or being attacked by something in the water. The federal government and Holt's family did not conduct an inquiry, as they believed his death was an accident. Some suggested Holt died by suicide, but police and his wife believed that was unlikely. Holt's disappearance fed numerous conspiracy theories, including Holt faking his own death to be with his lover, being assassinated by the CIA or North Vietnam, or defecting to China and being rescued via submarine. Ironically, a swimming center in Glen Iris, Melbourne, was named after Holt.

VANDINO AND UGOLINO VIVALDI

Vandino and Ugolino Vivaldi were Genoese brothers who were sea explorers and merchants in the 13th century. The Vivaldi brothers were believed to have been among the first explorers to attempt to find an ocean passage from Europe to India through Africa in what is now known as the Cape Route. The brothers commanded an expedition, funded by Tedisio Doria of the wealthy Doria family, that left Genoa in May 1291 with two armed galley ships. The purpose of the voyage was to trade with merchants in India as well as make an attempt at proselytism, the practice of trying to convert people to different religions, and two Franciscan friars went with the Vivaldis. The Vivaldi expedition sailed down the Morocco coast but was never seen again after stopping in Gozora, now known as Cape Nun.

It is believed that Genoese navigator Lancelotto Malocello searched for Vandino and Ugolino in 1312, as well as Ugolino's son, Sorleone de Vivaldo, who was denied entrance to Aksum by the King of Mogadishu due to an unsecure route. In 1455, Antoniotto Uso di Mare, another Genoese explorer, claimed to have met a descendant of the Vivaldi expedition. Mare claims that the man said the ships had reached the Sea of Guinea, where one of the ships was stranded, and the last ship was seized near what is now the Senegal River. Italian chronicler Galvano Fiamma claims that the Vivaldi expedition reached Ethiopia, where the surviving members eventually gave up the idea of returning home.

Historians believe that the friars that were aboard the expedition may have been influenced by *Opus Majus*, written by Roger Bacon, which incorrectly stated that Spain and India were not very far apart from each other. This could have led the Vivaldi brothers to take a route that would have gotten them stranded in an area they were not familiar with or prepared for. Other historians have posited that the Canary Island of Alegranza could have been named after the Vivaldi ship the *Alegranzia,* which would suggest that the expedition landed there. The Vivaldis are also alluded to in the travelogue *Libro del Conoscimiento*, written by an anonymous Spanish friar in the mid-14th century. In that book, there are two passages that seemingly talk about the Vivaldi brothers, which state that the two ships were separated in "Graciona" and "Magdasor," and which are believed to be evidence that points to the idea that the second ship was taken near the Horn of Africa.

There is no official evidence or conclusion regarding what happened to the Vivaldi brothers and their expedition, but their disappearance has sparked many legends, including being captured by the mythical Christian King Prester John, and it is believed to have been the inspiration for Dante's *Inferno*, in which Ulysses's last voyage fails in Canto 26.

THE BERMUDA TRIANGLE: SHIP MYSTERIES

Not only planes have vanished in the Bermuda Triangle—there are many reports over the years of ships vanishing without a trace. Here are two of the more mysterious examples.

The story of the *Ellen Austin*, if true, is one of the most chilling tales from Triangle lore. The *Ellen Austin* was a ship that sailed from London to New York in 1881. The trip was uneventful, until the ship came to an area of the Atlantic just north of the Bermuda Triangle.

There, the captain and crew spotted a schooner (a large sailing ship with masts) floating in the ocean. It seemed to be in good condition, but they saw no crew, and no one at all on board. The captain, suspicious that pirates might be lying in wait to ambush another passing ship, ordered his crew to observe the ship for a day or two. When nothing happened, he sent a salvage crew over, who confirmed that no one was on board, but that everything else—food, cargo, belongings, and so on—was. There was no sign of struggle; it just looked like everyone had abandoned ship for no reason.

The captain decided to guide the ship along with the *Ellen Austin*, and placed a small crew on it to operate it. But after two days, the ships got separated in a storm. The captain of the *Ellen Austin* went back to look for the other ship and found it again, drifting...and the crew he had placed on it was also now missing! A British navy officer, Commander Rupert Gould, recorded this story in 1944. He was a reliable researcher, but the source of his story is not fully known. If true, it's a very disturbing and unsettling tale indeed!

Another strange disappearance was that of the USS *Cyclops*, a large cargo ship that was sailing in March 1918 from the West Indies to Baltimore. It was 550 feet long and had a crew of more than 300. The trip was supposed to take nine days, but somewhere between Barbados and its destination (and somewhere in the Bermuda Triangle), it simply vanished. There were no SOS signals, no calls for help, simply a final message that said, "Weather fair, all well."

Perhaps German torpedoes attacked the ship? The United States had entered World War I, and the possibility of an attack was certainly something many thought of. But again, no debris was found (those kinds of attacks most often leave some objects floating on the surface), as well as little to no evidence that German forces had been in the area. *Santa Fe Magazine* wrote in 1920 that the ship "just disappeared as though some gigantic monster of the sea had grabbed her, men and all, and sent her into the depths of the ocean, and the suddenness of her destruction is amplified by the absence of any wireless calls for help being picked up by any ship along the route."

The US Navy later said of the incident: "The disappearance of this ship has been one of the most baffling mysteries in the annals of the Navy, all attempts to locate her having proved unsuccessful."

Like other vessels and people, the USS *Cyclops* just vanished.

THE BERMUDA TRIANGLE: EXPLANATIONS?

At least fifty ships and twenty planes have been lost in the area of the Bermuda Triangle over the past 100 years or so.

So, what's going on? Is there really something strange about this area that dooms so many vessels in the air and on the sea? Or is the Triangle's reputation simply the product of overactive imaginations, urban legends, and wishful thinking about UFOs, portals to another dimension, and more?

One explanation that some have favored is that the area may have a large bar magnet under the surface of the ocean floor. This could be a kind of naturally occurring magnet that changes in intensity over time. Is it possible that when this magnetic force is especially strong, it can mess with compasses, or even pull planes and ships into the ocean? It seems like an interesting idea, because so many have gone missing with no wreckage found. If a giant magnet were pulling them down, they'd sink to the ocean floor and never be seen again.

The USS *Cyclops* was carrying a large amount of ore for making steel when it vanished, so maybe something like this happened?

The problem is that no one can prove that such a powerful magnet exists.

Some skeptics have studied the area and asserted that there really haven't been that many more missing ships and planes in the region than elsewhere in the world, and that the reputation of the Bermuda Triangle is just scary and mystifying, so things get blown out of proportion.

A lot of the stories about missing ships and so on are just made up or exaggerated, they claim, and urban legends grow around the actual disappearances. Although this is true to a point about Flight 19, and maybe the *Ellen Austin* encounter, there is no doubt that the USS *Cyclops* and several other ships have indeed vanished without a trace. And why would the area gain a reputation for causing so many mysterious wrecks and disappearances, if they hadn't really happened?

At the other end, there are legends and tales of UFOs being seen over this stretch of sea, mysterious gateways to another world, and even the possibility that a piece of the lost continent of Atlantis lies underneath the waves in the Triangle, and that its ancient technologies and magic sometimes cause ships and planes to go haywire and disappear. This is all cool and fun stuff, but it's pretty hard, if not impossible, to prove.

It seems like there's something weird about the area of ocean known as the Bermuda Triangle, and for some reason, ships and planes sometimes just go missing when passing through. But no one knows yet what's actually causing it, and maybe we never will. If something mysterious is under the ocean out there, maybe we're better off not knowing?

GIOVANNI "JOHN" CABOT

John Cabot, Giovanni Caboto in Italian, was a navigator and explorer from Italy who was born around 1450. It is believed that Cabot began working in maritime trade around 1476, including participating in the slave trade. He married a woman named Mattea and had three sons: Ludovico, Sebastian, and Sancto.

It is believed that Cabot left Venice in 1488 as an insolvent debtor because he got into financial trouble. When he moved to Valencia, Spain, his creditors tried to have him arrested but were unsuccessful. He also fled to Seville, Spain, and Lisbon, Portugal, before reaching England around 1495. Cabot planned to find an alternative route to China, much like Christopher Columbus, and sought financing and a royal patent from England. He was issued a royal patent in 1496, most likely from Bristol, and was asked only to trade within England in hopes of making Bristol a monopoly port. Cabot received financial backing from tax collectors from the Italian community in London who introduced Cabot to King Henry VII.

It is believed that Cabot's first voyage was in the summer of 1496, but he did not make it. His second voyage had better documentation, on a small ship called *Matthew of Bristol* that departed in May 1497 with a crew of about twenty. Cabot sailed across the Atlantic, landing somewhere on the coast of North America in June 1497. The exact location they landed in is unknown but is believed to have been what is now Newfoundland. After returning to Bristol, Cabot reported his expedition to the king.

Cabot departed for his final voyage in May 1498 with a fleet of five ships with merchandise that included cloth, caps, lace points, and more. No other records on Cabot's travels were found for centuries, and it was widely believed that Cabot and his crew were lost at sea. However, one of the men that was supposed to be on the expedition is recorded to have lived in London in 1501. Historian Alwyn Ruddock studied Cabot for thirty-five years, and came to believe that Cabot's ship did return to England in the 1500s.

CHAPTER 5
DRIVING INTO THE ABYSS

MOST OF US HAVE EXPERIENCED the chilling quiet that comes when driving late at night. On a long stretch of road, with no other cars, people, or even lights around us, an eerie feeling settles in, like the world may have ended and somehow we've just kept on driving. On a seemingly endless road to nowhere, we are the only people left on Earth. For most of us, we arrive at our destinations, come home to family or friends, and reconnect with the world we'd temporarily been outside of. But for some, the road leads them in a darker direction. This chapter is about these people, those who got in their cars, drove off, and were never seen again.

JIM SULLIVAN

Jim Sullivan was a talented but relatively unknown singer-songwriter. You've probably never heard of him, and that's okay; a lot of people haven't. He wrote music that was a mix of folk, rock, and country, and although he showed promise, he struggled to become better known. He released an album in 1969 and another in 1972, but neither of these was particularly successful, and he was growing tired of playing clubs in Los Angeles and trying to make his way in show business. In 1975, with his marriage falling apart and his issues with alcohol worsening, he decided to pack up his things and drive to Nashville, thinking that he might have more success doing country music there than in California.

He left Los Angeles on March 3, 1975, driving a southern route that took him through Arizona and New Mexico. A highway patrolman remembers giving Sullivan a warning about his driving (it's easy to speed on those long, straight desert roads!), and on the following day, he checked into a motel in Santa Rosa, in central New Mexico.

But witnesses don't think he slept in the room overnight. The day after that, Sullivan's car was found at a ranch about twenty-six miles away from Santa Rosa, and a few people say they saw him walking away from it, but didn't really pay any attention. Inside the car were his money, guitar, extra clothes, copies of records, and other materials. It was the last time anyone would ever see Sullivan. A search was conducted, but nothing was ever found. Although he had been depressed about his career in Los Angeles, he seemed genuinely interested in trying again in Nashville, so it makes no sense. And if he were trying to kill himself, there would have been easier ways to do it.

One part of the story, however, made many think there might be more to it than just his disappearance. His first album from 1969 was called *U.F.O.*, and on it, he had lyrics about driving on desert highways, about leaving everything behind...and about being abducted by a UFO! Was his trip to Nashville just a cover for something else? Did he really think he could walk out into the wild and a UFO would come to take him? Perhaps he was suffering from a breakdown, and he just abandoned everything in hopes that aliens would take him away if he went out to them. The area he disappeared in is not all that far from Roswell (the site of an infamous suspected UFO incident). Did he do it on purpose? Maybe he thought he would be rescued by aliens and died out there somewhere, but if so, why was a body never found?

Or...what if he knew he was going to be found and arranged to meet someone, or something, out there? Was he taken away to another world, one that he thought would be better for him?

CHARLES AND CATHERINE ROMER

Charles Romer was a wealthy man in the oil business who lived with his wife, Catherine, in New York City. But, because both were in their seventies, they preferred to go south for the winter—in this case, to Florida, where they had an apartment and could spend the colder months in the warmth of Miami. In 1980, they stayed in Miami until April. On April 8, they set off for New York, with the intention of being back there by April 10. They stopped in Georgia, in a town called Brunswick, and checked into a Holiday Inn in the afternoon. They left a little while later to have dinner in town, and a highway patrolman recalled seeing their distinctive black car; it was a 1979 Lincoln Continental Town Car, with a customized license plate that read, "CRR-CBR," the couple's initials. And that was the last time anyone ever saw them.

When they didn't turn up at their home two days later, and the hotel maids noticed that they hadn't been sleeping in their bed, a search commenced. Their hotel room still had their luggage and some valuable jewelry, proof that they hadn't actually left the area intentionally. The roads were searched, all the way back to the Florida border, and their son hired a private investigator, but nothing turned up.

One theory was that they'd lost control of the car in the dark and driven into one of the rivers or swamps in the area. An experienced local diver, George

Baker, committed himself to the search for the car, but after making more than 300 dives, he found nothing, not even a clue of its whereabouts.

Some years later, a woman remembered her husband saying he had been run off the road by a vehicle matching the description of the Romers' car, but she couldn't provide much in the way of details.

Maybe the Romers had been robbed, or even murdered, and the killer had taken off in their car. This seems like a possibility, but the car itself was never found, and neither were the bodies of Charles or Catherine. George Baker even did some extra diving in the area where the incident was supposed to have happened, but found nothing.

As one law enforcement official said, it was as if they had vanished off the face of the earth. To this day, no trace of them has ever been found, and the case is still technically open and unsolved in Georgia.

EDWARD AND STEPHANIA ANDREWS

The Andrewses weren't having a good time at the party. It was May 1970, and they were at a business function at the Sheraton Hotel in downtown Chicago, having arrived there at about 6:15 p.m.

Edward said he felt rather ill, and blamed it on the fact that there was nothing much to eat and that he was really hungry. So he was drinking alcohol instead, which, on an empty stomach, just made him feel worse. In any case, the couple stayed until about 9:30 p.m., and then set off for their home, which wasn't that far away in Arlington Heights, a suburb northwest of Chicago.

Witnesses said that Edward looked unwell, and Stephania seemed like she'd been crying. Had they argued? What was wrong? The parking attendant remembered that Edward scraped the car's fender against the exit door, but kept right on driving. Strangely, Edward turned the wrong way onto a one-way street. Clearly, something was wrong with him; he was either drunk, or feeling very ill, or both.

Whatever the problem was, that attendant was the last person to see them. Stephania and Edward never made it home, and they were never found. Almost immediately, theories started emerging. It turned out that Edward had lunch with his brother earlier in the day, and was already complaining of feeling ill then. So perhaps Edward was either drunk or had a heart attack, and had driven his car off a bridge. The car might have plunged into the Chicago River, which seemed like a good possibility, but a search of the bridges revealed no sign of an accident, and a sweep of the river didn't locate their car. Some theorized that the car might have gone over and been carried out to Lake Michigan by the current, which is why no one could find it in the river, but again, there was no sign of a car going off the road anywhere.

The Andrewses simply vanished somewhere between Chicago and Arlington Heights. A police search of their home turned up nothing unusual, and there were no reports of credit cards or bank accounts being tampered with. So, the idea that their car plunged into the river seems the most likely, but why was there no evidence of it? No trace of the Andrewses or their car has ever been found.

BRANDON SWANSON

Nineteen-year-old Brandon Swanson was celebrating the conclusion of his first year of college in Minnesota on the evening of May 14, 2008. He'd had a good time out and was on his way home, when for some reason, he acci-dentally drove his car into a ditch. He wasn't hurt, but he was stuck. So he did the sensible thing and called his parents, asking if they could come and pick him up. Of course, Annette and Brian Swanson said they would be over as soon as they could. His parents hopped in their truck and headed out to where their son said he was, which was only about ten minutes away. They had him on the phone when they arrived, but they didn't see anything.

They tried flashing their lights, and told him on the phone they were doing so. Brandon said he was flashing his, but neither of them saw each other. Clearly, Brandon was not where he thought he was.

Brandon announced that he would walk back to the nearby town of Lynd, and asked his parents to meet him in the parking lot of a nightclub there. His father dropped his mother off at home and headed out again. Father and son kept talking on the phone, but at some point, Brandon swore and the line went dead. His dad tried calling him over and over, but there was no answer.

No one ever saw Brandon again.

His parents stayed out all night looking for him, and by morning, the police were involved. They eventually found Brandon's car, stuck in a ditch as he had said on the phone, but twenty-five miles away from Lynd. His cell phone calls were also traced to a local tower. There were no signs that anything was wrong, so he must have believed he really was close to home and was starting back to Lynd, like he said he was going to. Search dogs were brought in and caught a scent, which led down an old gravel road to an abandoned farm, but they weren't able to find any sign of him, and the trail went cold. There were no signs of clothing, his phone, anything. Brandon vanished into the night.

So many questions remain. How did Brandon get so off course? He knew the area, so why did he think he was close to home when he was driving in a completely different direction and twenty-five miles away? He clearly thought he was still close to Lynd and could walk back to a nightclub there... why? He didn't sound like he was under the influence of drugs or alcohol on the phone. Did he experience missing time? Why did he swear just as the line went dead? What did he see? Why did his trail lead toward an old farm and then go cold? Did something beyond this known world take him?

LEAH ROBERTS

Leah Roberts was a fun and easygoing college student, though she'd had some difficult times too. In the 1990s, she went through several upsetting events: her dad suffered a serious illness that eventually killed him, and her mom died of heart disease. Then, Leah was in car accident and needed surgery, and a metal rod was put in her leg to help it heal. At the time, she was studying at North Carolina State University, but the accident did something to her. She felt lucky to be alive, and had a new sense of purpose and a desire to live life fully. After her dad died, she decided to leave school for a while and find herself. She moved in with her friend Nicole in Durham, North Carolina, and for a while, everything seemed okay.

But on March 9, 2000, everything changed.

That day, Roberts spoke with her sister, Kara, about meeting up and told Nicole that she'd help her babysit the following night. When Nicole came home later, she saw that Roberts's Jeep was gone, but didn't think much of it, because she was out a lot anyway. But when Roberts didn't show up the following day, Nicole and Kara became worried and reported her missing. When they searched her room, they found a note that said, "I'm not suicidal. I'm the opposite." She also left money for rent and bills, and had taken a lot of clothes and other things. Clearly, she was being spontaneous and had decided to go on a trip somewhere to get away. She was obviously intending to return...except, she never did.

Her sister was able to trace Leah to a town called Brooks in Oregon, so she'd driven all the way across the United States! For the moment, Kara and Nicole were just glad she was safe. But on March 18, which was Kara's birthday, her sister didn't call, which was not like her at all. Instead, she got a phone call from the sheriff's office in Bellingham, Washington, north of Seattle and near the Canadian border.

Leah Roberts's Jeep had been found in a ravine in a very wooded area. It had been driven off the road and had crashed below. This was awful news, but it was about to become very strange.

Leah was nowhere to be found, but the Jeep still had her credit cards, passport, ID, and about $2,500 in cash in the pocket of a pair of jeans. There was no blood inside, and no evidence that anyone had been in the vehicle when it ran off the road. Even weirder, there were pillows inside and blankets hung across the windows, suggesting it had been used as a shelter after the crash. Police searched the area extensively, but didn't find Leah or any sign of her. One theory was that she might have been slightly hurt in the crash and stayed in the Jeep for a day or two, and then climbed back up to the road and tried to get help, but was abducted and killed somewhere else. It turns out she'd been in the area at least five days before the car was found. Several people saw her sitting in a food court, talking with two guys she'd met there. One of them told police that Roberts left with another man named "Barry." Unfortunately, no one else remembered seeing him, including the other man who chatted with her. Nothing came of any of it, until 2006, when a new investigator reexamined the case. In looking at the Jeep, he discovered that the starter relay had been cut, which would allow the Jeep to accelerate without actually being driven. So the crash probably was staged!

The man who insisted she left with "Barry" was a mechanic; could he have done it? A fingerprint under the hood and DNA found on Roberts's clothes didn't match his, so he was ruled out. There were no other leads, and "Barry" has never been identified. Where is she, and what happened to her? Unfortunately, the case has gone cold and is still a mystery.

MAURA MURRAY

The case of Maura Murray is especially strange, because according to the evidence, she didn't wander off from somewhere; she just disappeared. Murray was twenty-one and a good student. She was studying nursing and doing well. On the night of February 9, 2004, she was driving her car in snowy weather near Woodsville, New Hampshire, when she lost control and drove into a snowbank, an all-too-common thing in New England at that time of year.

Another driver passed by, and slowed to ask if she needed help. She seemed okay, and said no, she had already called for roadside assistance. The driver went on his way, assuming all was fine. About ten minutes later, the police arrived to help, but when they got there, Maura's car was locked, and she was gone.

There were no tracks in the snow, and dogs as well as an aerial search didn't reveal anything. As investigators began to look into the case, they started noticing some odd things. She had removed nearly $300 from her bank account and had emailed a teacher saying she was going to miss class because there had been a death in the family.

Except there hadn't been, so why was Maura lying? She had apparently bought a lot of alcohol before setting off, but that wasn't in the trunk. There was a box of wine that had broken open, presumably during the crash, and a soda bottle that smelled like it had alcohol in it, so she might have been drinking while driving, which could have made her lose control.

A search of records revealed that she called a resort in New Hampshire shortly before leaving, so she obviously had some sort of plan, but what was it? Was she planning a secret getaway on her own or with friends, and wanted to skip class to do it? Maybe, but then, how and why did she disappear? Other questions began to emerge.

It seemed that the damage to her car could not have been caused by simply driving into snow, meaning it had to have been damaged before. And a rag was stuffed into the gas pipe of the car, which a person might do to either damage it, or to hide the fact that it was already damaged from the highway patrol.

Some have suspected that another person was in the car, maybe in the backseat, maybe crouched down when the other driver stopped to ask if she needed help. It was already getting dark by then, and a second person could probably have hidden pretty easily. Maybe it was a coordinated kidnapping: this second person abducted her at gunpoint and forced her to drive gently into a snowbank, and then a second driver came along minutes later. They took the alcohol and drove off in another car, taking Murray with them. This would explain why there was no sign of her in the surrounding area, and why there were no footprints in the snow leading away.

But what really happened to her? In her dorm room, her belongings were found packed into boxes, showing that she intended to leave for some reason. Did her plan to sneak off go horribly wrong? To this day, no one knows.

FELIPE SANTOS AND TERRANCE WILLIAMS

Felipe Santos and Terrance Williams were two men who went missing under similar circumstances in 2003 and 2004, respectively, in Naples, Florida.

Originally from Tennessee, Terrance Williams was a father of four and moved to Florida to be closer to his mother, Marcia. On January 11, 2004, Williams's roommate says he spoke with Williams on the phone on January 11, 2004, after Williams attended a party at his coworkers' house. At the time, Williams did not have a valid driver's license, due to being charged with a DUI; unable to find a ride, Williams drove illegally to the party but never returned home.

Terrance's family filed a missing persons report on January 13 and tracked down his car, which had been towed for obstructing traffic. They found that the tow report was signed by Deputy Steve Calkins from the Collier County Sheriff's Department, but Calkins had not made an arrest or filed an incident report. Marcia contacted workers at a nearby cemetery, and they allegedly saw Calkins pat down Terrance and drive away with him. Calkins asked the employees of the cemetery if he could leave Williams's car there, but returned within the hour to move it to the side of the road, where the car keys were found on the ground.

The Williams family demanded to speak to Calkins, but the deputy denied having any memory of arresting Williams. After his supervisors asked him to submit an incident report, Calkins stated that he noticed Terrance's car being driven "in distress" and pulled him over. Calkins claimed that

Williams asked for a ride to the Circle K convenience store because he was late for his shift (Terrance did not work there) and Calkins dropped him off. Calkins also claimed that Terrance had told him the car's registration papers were in the glove compartment, but he did not find them; he then called the Circle K, where the clerk told him that Williams did not work there. No calls, witnesses, or security footage support Calkins's claims.

Marcia filed a complaint against Calkins and was contacted by the Mexican Consulate in Miami, who told her that another man disappeared under similar circumstances a year prior.

Felipe Santos was a Mexican citizen living in Immokalee, Florida, for three years, sending money back to his family. On October 14, 2003, Santos was driving in Naples with his two brothers when he got into a minor car accident. Calkins cited him for driving without a license or insurance and reckless driving. The last time Santos was seen was when Calkins drove away with him in his patrol car. Later that day, Santos's boss contacted the county jail to post bail but found that Santos had never been booked. Calkins claimed he changed his mind about arresting Santos and said he left him at a Circle K (a different location from the Williams case).

Two weeks later, Calkins submitted an incident report. The Santos family simultaneously filed a missing persons report for Felipe and an official complaint against Calkins. Calkins was cleared of any suspicion in the Santos case. In 2004, it was found that Calkins's recorded call with dispatch revealed more conflicting statements from the officer, including the fact that he knew Williams's name when he originally claimed he did not.

The Florida Department of Law Enforcement and the FBI were called in to investigate, and Calkins was fired from the department for providing false information and failing to cooperate with both investigations, although no physical evidence turned up to prove Calkins was involved in either man's disappearance.

One popular theory is that Calkins was engaging in the starlight tour phenomenon: a police practice that originated in Canada, where police would drive individuals outside the city limits and abandon them to find their own way home. This practice came to light in 2000, when several

Indigenous Canadians were abducted and left abandoned in the wilderness in Saskatoon, Saskatchewan, Canada. Neither Santos nor Williams has been heard from since their disappearances. No arrests have been made.

BRIANNA MAITLAND

Brianna Maitland was an American teenager who went missing when she was seventeen. Prior to her disappearance, Maitland decided in October 2003 that she wanted to move out of her parents' farm in East Franklin, Vermont. Maitland enrolled in her friends' school, but by February 2004 she dropped out of high school after living in several different homes belonging to her friends. That month, she moved in with her childhood friend, Jillian Stout, in Sheldon, Vermont, and enrolled in a GED program. Less than a month before she went missing, Maitland was attacked by a former friend, Kaellie Lacross, which resulted in Maitland suffering a broken nose and a concussion. Maitland pressed charges, and witnesses stated that Maitland did not fight back, despite being trained in martial arts.

On March 19, 2004, Maitland got lunch with her mother, Kellie. As the pair were shopping, Brianna was distracted by something outside and left her mother. After meeting her in the parking lot, Kellie noticed Brianna seemed agitated and scared, and Brianna asked her mother to drop her off at Stout's home to get ready for her shift at the Black Lantern Inn in nearby Montgomery. Maitland clocked out of work at 11:20 p.m., and told her coworkers she had a shift at her second job in the morning. Witnesses all state that she was alone in the car when she left.

On March 20, a Vermont State Police trooper found Maitland's car at an empty house off Route 118 in Richford. Believing it to have been abandoned by a drunk driver, the trooper called a towing company. At the scene, loose change, a water bottle, and an unsmoked cigarette were found.

Due to her scattered lifestyle and miscommunication, Maitland was not reported missing for several days. Her mother only learned of her car being abandoned five days after it was discovered. On March 23, her mother filed a missing persons report. Vermont police originally believed her to be a runaway, but Maitland's father noted that her debit card, contact lenses, and migraine medication were still in the car.

Two anonymous tips to police pointed suspicion to local drug dealers Ramon L. Ryans and Nathaniel Charles Jackson, whom Maitland's friends claim she was associated with. A signed affidavit from an anonymous woman claimed that Ryans murdered Maitland over money he lent her and disposed of her body on a pig farm. Maitland's parents received several anonymous phone calls that stated that she was tied to a tree or at the bottom of a lake. None of these claims have been corroborated by law enforcement.

In 2006, security footage of an Atlantic City casino went viral due to a woman's resemblance to Brianna, but police were unable to identify the woman. In 2012, investigators ruled out serial killer Israel Keyes, who committed numerous rapes and murders in Alaska, Oregon, Washington, New York, and Vermont. In 2016, investigators announced they had recovered DNA samples from Maitland's car, but the results were not made publicly available. In March 2022, police said they had found a match to the DNA that belonged to one of eleven people previously tested.

RAY GRICAR

Ray Gricar was an American lawyer who served as the district attorney of Centre County, Pennsylvania, from 1985 to 2005. After graduating from college, Gricar studied law at Case Western Reserve University School of Law, where he obtained his Juris Doctor and specialized in prosecuting rape and murder charges in Cuyahoga County, Ohio. In 1980, Gricar, his first wife, and his daughter, Lana, moved to State College, Pennsylvania, where he eventually ran for district attorney. Gricar divorced his wife and again in 1996 before getting divorced again five years later. At the time of his disappearance, he was living with his girlfriend, Patty Fornicola, in her childhood home in Bellefonte, Pennsylvania.

In May 1996, Gricar's older brother, Roy, disappeared from his home in West Chester, Ohio, and was found in the Great Miami River; he had died by suicide.

At 11:30 a.m. on April 15, 2005, Gricar called Fornicola to tell her he was on his way home, but when he did not return, she reported him missing. The next day, investigators found Gricar's red Mini Cooper in the parking lot of an antique store adjacent to the Susquehanna River. The car contained his work-issued cell phone but not his laptop, keys, or wallet. Police dogs did not find a scent of him in the river, but investigators believe that he may have gotten into another person's car.

On July 30, fisherman found his work-issued laptop in the river, but its hard drive was missing. In September, the hard drive was discovered 100 yards from where the laptop was found, but investigators were unable to find anything from data recovery. It was later revealed that someone in Gricar's home had searched "how to wreck a hard drive" and "water damage to a notebook computer" before he went missing.

In June 2011, Gricar's daughter petitioned to have him declared dead in absentia.

There are three main theories in Gricar's disappearance: suicide, murder, and that he fled his life for a new one. Police believe that Gricar committed suicide due to the similarities between his disappearance and his brother's; however, Gricar had no history of depression or suicidal thoughts and had expressed to family that he was excited for retirement. Some believe Gricar's death could be related to the unsolved death of Assistant US Attorney Jonathan Luna or his decision not to prosecute Penn State football coach Jerry Sandusky, or even a police operation he had been involved in that busted a heroin dealing ring.

A third theory is that Gricar faked his own disappearance due to an alleged interest in a Cleveland police chief who disappeared to start a new life.

Many people have reported sightings of Gricar after he went missing, one of which was a bartender and an off-duty police officer who claimed to have seen Gricar watching a baseball game in a bar in Wilkes-Barre, Pennsylvania. Some believe he moved to central Europe because he was fluent in Slovenian and semifluent in Russian, and had family in Slovenia.

JAMIE FRALEY

Jamie Fraley was a twenty-two-year-old who went missing in 2008 while en route to the hospital. At the time of her disappearance, Fraley was attending Gaston College part-time, with plans to become a substance-abuse counselor after graduation. According to family, Fraley had struggled with anxiety and bipolar disorder in her early life, but by the time she disappeared, she was on prescription medication and was doing well. In 2006, Fraley began dating Ricky Simonds Jr., and they soon became engaged. Simonds had a criminal history of petty crimes and was sentenced to fifteen months in prison for theft in 2007, but Fraley continued to visit him while he was incarcerated.

On April 7, 2008, Fraley suffered from a stomach virus for which she sought treatment at a local hospital twice that day. Fraley did not have a driver's license, so she relied on friends, family, and a social worker to drive her to and from the hospital. After the first trip, one of Fraley's friends visited her and dropped off her prescription at the drugstore. Ricky Simonds Sr., her fiancé's father, who lived in the same apartment complex as a maintenance worker, drove her to the hospital and another neighbor drove her back. At around midnight, Fraley called her mother to tell her she was going back to the hospital. On April 8, she called a friend in Albemarle at 1:30 a.m. and mentioned she was going back to the hospital but did not elaborate on who was driving her; however, she did refer to the driver as "he."

When Fraley failed to appear at an important meeting the next day, her family checked on her apartment. The door was locked, but inside they found that her cell phone was missing; her wallet, identification, purse, and keys remained in the apartment. There was no sign of a struggle, but after being unable to reach her, her family reported her missing to Gaston County police.

The Gaston County police launched a huge investigation, with help from the FBI and the North Carolina Bureau of Investigation. Two days after her disappearance, utility workers found her phone about a mile from her apartment. Fraley's fiancé was still incarcerated at the time of her disappearance, so he was ruled out as a suspect, but his father, Simonds Sr., was a person of interest, due to the fact that he lived two doors down from Fraley and served six years in prison for manslaughter after strangling his girlfriend to death in 1980. According to reports, Simonds Sr. was obsessed with Fraley and had driven her to the hospital earlier that day, but he refused to take a lie detector test. Two months to the day after Fraley disappeared, Simonds Sr. was found dead in the trunk of the car belonging to his ex-girlfriend, Kim Sprenger. Sprenger had filed a protective order against him, and it was believed that Simonds Sr. was planning on ambushing her but had suffered from heat exhaustion and died from accidental heatstroke.

Both Fraley's family and Simonds Jr. believe that Simonds Sr. had information about Fraley's disappearance.

TONI SHARPLESS

Toni Sharpless was an American woman who disappeared after leaving a party in 2009. Sharpless, born and raised in the suburbs of Philadelphia, worked at Lancaster General Hospital as a nurse. Throughout her life, Sharpless struggled with bipolar disorder and drug and alcohol abuse.

On August 22, 2009, Sharpless met up with her friend Crystal Johns and went to a club in Center City in downtown Philadelphia, and later went to a party at NBA player Willie Green's house. They left Center City at around 3:00 a.m. on August 23. Sharpless responded to a text from her daughter at 2:57 a.m., and the phone was ultimately turned off around 4:00 a.m. At the party, the group began playing the board game *Taboo*, when Sharpless reportedly made a remark to Johns that caused Green to become offended. Sharpless felt that the other guests were ridiculing her and became erratic and angry at approximately 5:00 a.m., Sharpless allegedly dumped a bottle of champagne on the floor and began kicking things in the kitchen. Green told Johns and Sharpless to leave.

Johns tried to take the car keys from Sharpless, but Sharpless insisted that she drive, although she was much drunker than Johns. During the drive, Johns asked Sharpless if she should be driving drunk after getting a DUI, in addition to the fact that she had been awake for over thirty-six hours straight. Sharpless immediately stopped the car and demanded that Johns get out, which she did. Sharpless then drove off, never to be seen again. Johns waited for her to return, and called Toni's sister, Candy Sharpless, to complain, but learned that Toni had not returned home. Johns then called the police, and Candy later filed a missing persons report.

Police originally believed Sharpless had accidently driven down a boat ramp into the Schuylkill River, but sonar did not locate her car. Two weeks after Sharpless's disappearance, an automated license plate reader found a hit on Sharpless's car in Camden, New Jersey, across the Delaware River from Philadelphia. The Camden Police Department did not alert local authorities until a few days later, and they were unable to find the vehicle.

Sharpless's mother, Donna Knebel, hired private investigator Eileen Law to investigate her disappearance, and Law set up a website and hotline number dedicated to tips from the public about Sharpless. Law came to believe that Sharpless may have driven toward Camden due to her inebriated state and run out of gas, becoming stranded without any money on her person.

In December 2012, Law received an anonymous letter postmarked from Trenton, New Jersey, from a "Tony Sharpless," that claimed that they had been offered $5,000 to take Sharpless's car to a shop in Boston and asked if they knew anyone in need of a "paper-trip," a term referring to getting a new identity and Social Security card. The writer claimed that a Camden police officer had gotten into a fight with a woman and needed the car moved out of state. The writer kept the license plates and Social Security card in a box and also said they found Sharpless's phone and wrote down the VIN number. The writer proved the account by including the license plate number, VIN, and Social Security number; the last two numbers on the license plate number had not been made public, but the writer got it correct.

Sharpless's family continues to believe that Johns made up her version of the night in order to cover up an accident that occurred inside the party, but police cleared Johns of any involvement, as well as all the guests at the party.

JIMMY HOFFA

Jimmy Hoffa was an American labor union leader and former president of the International Brotherhood of Teamsters, where he helped union workers get better wages. As a Teamster, Hoffa became involved with organized crime and the Mafia. In 1964, he was convicted of jury tampering, attempted bribery, conspiracy, and mail and wire fraud. He resigned as union president in 1971 after an agreement with President Richard Nixon in exchange for a lesser sentence. He was barred from union activity until 1980.

After getting out of prison, Hoffa tried to find support within the Mafia to regain his position in the Teamsters; however, Anthony Provenzano, another Teamster leader, threatened Hoffa with a reprisal if he were to try to regain support. Two members of the Detroit Mafia, Anthony and Vito Giacalone, visited Hoffa under the guise of mediating a meeting between Hoffa and Provenzano. Hoffa's son believes this was the beginning of a plan to take a hit on his father. It is believed that Hoffa could have given investigators information that the Mafia was involved with the Teamsters, which could have prompted the Mob to kill off Hoffa.

On July 30, 1975, Hoffa went to the Machus Red Fox restaurant in a suburb of Detroit, where he was set to meet Anthony Giacalone and Anthony Provenzano. Around 2:30 p.m., after arriving at the restaurant, he called his wife to complain that the men were late, and stated he would be home at 4:00 p.m. Witnesses reported that Hoffa got in a car with three other people and left around 2:50 p.m. Hoffa was never seen again.

The next morning, investigators found Hoffa's car unlocked in the Red Fox parking lot, with no indication of what had happened to him. The main piece of physical evidence was Provenzano's son's car, which matched the description of the car witnesses saw Hoffa sitting in on the day of his disappearance. The car had been borrowed by Charles O'Brien, Hoffa's foster son, with whom he had an icy relationship, to deliver fish. Police canines found Hoffa's scent in the car. There were witnesses who stated they believed the man driving the car was O'Brien, but he denied any involvement.

Giacalone and Provenzano both claimed they had never set up a meeting with Hoffa, and both men had alibis: Giacalone was at the Southfield Athletic Club, and Provenzano was in New Jersey with his brother, gambling in a union hall. It is believed that these alibis were planned in order to deter investigation into their involvement.

Although investigators are confident in their ideas of who was involved in Hoffa's disappearance—and most likely murder—they will never be prosecuted, in order to protect informants and because of the lack of physical evidence. The case remains open, and Hoffa's body has yet to be found.

CHAPTER 6

YOUTH STOLEN: CHILDREN, TEENAGERS, AND STUDENTS

WHAT COULD POSSIBLY BE MORE terrifying than the loss of our children? Vulnerable and naive, children are inherently at a greater risk of going missing. For many years, adults have put more and more measures in place to try to prevent our precious young ones from wandering off or being taken. Children are taught not to speak to strangers, and not to leave their guardian's side. And yet how often does a parent find themselves turning back after looking away for only a moment, to find that their child is gone? How many teenagers sneak out of the house without anyone ever knowing? This chapter tells the tragic stories of young children, teenagers, and students who never came home.

ASHA DEGREE

Young Asha Degree walked out of her house in the early hours of February 14, 2000. Her family never saw her again. Asha was nine years old and lived with her family in a home outside of Shelby, North Carolina. She was a typical girl of her age, but tended to be a bit shy and quiet, and was scared of dogs. She wasn't trouble to her parents, though, and mostly seemed very happy and content.

On the night of February 13, the power in the neighborhood went out for a while, but came back on after midnight. Asha's father, Harold, checked in on her and her brother; they shared a bedroom and were sleeping. He checked in again at about 2:30 a.m., and sure enough, they were both sleeping soundly. But sometime not long after that, her brother said he was woken up by a squeak coming from Asha's bed. At the time, he thought she was just turning over, and he went back to sleep. When their mother came to wake them up at about 6:30 a.m. to get ready for school, Asha wasn't there. She wasn't anywhere in the house, or at her grandmother's across the street. Of course, her parents panicked. Then things got even stranger.

Asha had packed up some of her favorite belongings and clothes and left with them, so this was clearly not a kidnapping. For whatever reasons, she had planned this. Obviously, the first thought was that she was a runaway, but nothing at home would have made her want to leave. Interestingly, she was reading a book at school about children who have adventures after running away. Was she trying to do the same thing? If so, how long had she been planning it?

More clues came in. A truck driver and another motorist told police they had seen a girl matching Asha's description walking along the highway between 3:45 and 4:15 a.m. that morning. It had been pouring down rain, and they were concerned about her. The second motorist said that he turned his car around to go back and talk to her, or try to help her. But as he circled, she must have seen him, because she ran off into the woods, and that was the last time anyone saw her. The following day, some candy wrappers, a pencil, a marker, and a hair bow belonging to Asha were found near the spot where she was seen running into the woods.

A massive search was launched, but they found no other clues until more than a year later, in August 2001. Her book bag was found off the freeway, about twenty-six miles north of Shelby. It was wrapped in a plastic bag, but the strange thing was that it contained a book and a T-shirt that were not hers. The book came from her school's library.

After this, no other clues have been found, and she's still missing more than twenty years later.

What would make a nine-year-old get up in the middle of a terrible rainstorm and just walk away from her home and family? Why did she run into the woods, and why did no one find her? How did her bag get so far away, and why was there a library book and T-shirt in it that didn't belong to her? No one knows the answers to these questions, and despite all the time spent looking for her, there's been no trace of her anywhere.

THOMAS DEAN GIBSON

Thomas Dean Gibson was an American child who disappeared at age two from his front yard in Azalea, Oregon.

Around 11:30 a.m. on March 18, 1991, Gibson was playing in the front yard when his father, Larry Gibson, a sheriff's deputy in Douglas County, went for a jog. Gibson's four-year-old older sister, Karen, was supposed to watch him. Larry claimed he tried to shoot a stray cat but missed. When Larry returned forty-five minutes later, Thomas was missing.

Larry and his wife, Judith, reported Thomas missing to police and Larry was asked not to report that day; however, it is believed that Larry left the property in his uniform for approximately twenty-five minutes during the initial search, claiming that he went to a nearby rest area to search for Thomas. Karen, according to Larry, saw a couple pull into the driveway and abduct Thomas. Larry's patrol car was not searched the day of Thomas's disappearance, but authorities later found that the odometer in Larry's patrol car registered seven miles that were unaccounted for; Larry claimed that this was due to him searching the nearby rest area.

In 1992, Larry resigned from the Douglas County Sheriff's Office, and the family moved to Avon, Montana. After having another daughter, Judith and Larry separated. Judith and the children moved back to Oregon, while Larry moved to Townsend in Montana and became an insurance agent.

In 1994, Karen told police she witnessed Larry beating Thomas and putting him in his patrol car the morning of his disappearance. Larry was arrested in April 1994 for second-degree murder and extradited to Oregon. Larry's trial began in 1995, and his half sister, Debbie Calek, testified that Larry had confessed to killing Thomas. Calek also testified that Judith and Karen stayed with her in Iowa after the disappearance, where Karen said she was afraid of her father "putting her in a big hole" like he did with Thomas. Karen also testified against her father, saying Larry had threatened her and she did not feel safe telling authorities what she saw until her mother separated from him. Prosecutors alleged that Thomas had followed Larry during his jog, and after attempting to kill a cat, Larry carried Thomas to their carport and slapped him repeatedly, then hid Thomas's body in a plastic bag in the trunk of his vehicle and disposed of it in Swamp Creek while volunteers searched for Thomas.

Larry was convicted of manslaughter in 1995 and was released from prison a year later. Larry maintained his innocence and started a website in 2001, asking for public assistance to find his son. Thomas's body was never found.

ANDREW GOSDEN

Andrew Gosden disappeared from Central London at age fourteen after withdrawing £200 from his bank account. Gosden was a student at McAuley Catholic High School and was a part of the Young, Gifted & Talented Programme. Gosden was described by family as quiet and introverted, but not antisocial, as he had a small group of friends.

On September 14, 2007, Gosden had trouble waking up, and his mother stated that he seemed irritable, which was unusual since he usually woke up on time. Gosden was seen by Rev. Alan Murray, who stated that he saw him go to a cash machine, where he withdrew £200 out of the £214 in his account at around 8:05 a.m. CCTV footage captured Gosden returning home. At home, Gosden changed out of his uniform into casual clothes, left £100 in cash in his room, and took his wallet, keys, and PlayStation Portable console. Gosden did not bring his passport, a phone, or a charger for the PSP. At 8:30 a.m., Gosden left his house and purchased a one-way ticket to London, costing £31.40. At 9:35 a.m., Gosden was seen boarding a train to King's Cross Station alone and arrived at 11:20 a.m., where he was seen on CCTV footage leaving the station.

The school tried to contact the Gosdens to tell them that Andrew had not come into school, but misdialed the number. At dinner, his family discovered he was not home and called some of his friends, who informed them that he had not been at school. Authorities were called at 7:00 p.m.

Gosden's father believed the one-way ticket was not strange, as they had many relatives and friends in London. No evidence was found in either Gosden's neighborhood or neighborhoods in London where he may have visited, and no suspicious online activity of Gosden's was found. Authorities investigated several potential reasons for Gosden going to London, but no evidence was located to point in any one direction. Hundreds of sightings and tips have been reported to police, but none have turned up any solid leads to Gosden's whereabouts.

The Gosden family had many theories about Gosden's disappearance, one of which was that he was struggling with his sexual orientation; Gosden's father made a public plea for help from the gay community. The Gosden family has not changed the locks of their home in hopes that Gosden will return with the key he left with.

In December 2021, authorities arrested two men under suspicion for kidnapping, human trafficking, and child pornography, and these are thought to be the first arrests in connection to Gosden's disappearance. Another teenager, Alexander Sloley, disappeared ten months after Gosden in similar circumstances, and some believe the disappearances are connected.

MADELEINE McCANN

Madeleine McCann was a British child who disappeared in Portugal in 2007, in one of the most heavily reported-on missing persons cases in the 21st century.

The McCann family, along with a group of family friends and their children, arrived in Praia da Luz, Portugal, on April 28, 2007. They were staying in a privately owned ground-floor apartment next door to three other families they were vacationing with at the Ocean Club. The apartment was easily accessible from the street as well as the rest of the complex. On the morning of May 3, Madeleine asked her parents why they didn't come in when she and her brother were crying, and her mother noticed a strange brown stain on her pajamas; after her disappearance, her parents wondered if the kidnapper had been in the room the previous night.

That night, the McCanns put their children to sleep at 7:00 p.m. At 8:30 p.m., the McCann parents left to eat with their friends at the Ocean Club, which was about 100 yards away from the apartment. The McCanns left the doors unlocked with the curtains drawn and periodically checked in on the children. Madeleine's mother intended to check on the children at 9:30 p.m., but their friend Matthew Oldfield offered to do it while he checked on his children next door. Oldfield noticed their bedroom door was

wide open but didn't look to see if the children were there because he heard no noise. At 10:00 p.m., Madeleine's mother checked on the children and found Madeleine missing.

Due to mistakes made by investigators in the first hours of Madeleine's disappearance and the subsequent media circus perpetuated by the McCann family and the British government, there was much confusion and potentially lost physical evidence. It was also discovered that the resort staff left a note in a message book at the pool reception area that stated that the McCanns and their friends reserved the table that overlooked the apartments, which the McCanns believe the abductor saw. Investigators also searched the McCanns' apartment and rental car, with no evidence recovered.

The McCann family suffered scrunity from police and media that believed they had some involvement in Madeleine's disappearance, but the family insists that they were followed by a man while they were at the resort, and in January 2008, they released sketches of the man they believed took Madeleine. In 2011, the McCanns released a book about Madeleine and her disappearance.

The investigation by the Portuguese government closed in July 2008, but Scotland Yard opened a formal investigation in 2013. Scotland Yard identified around forty-one potential suspects at the time of the case being opened, and traveled to Portugal to interview them and investigate further. In 2022, a new suspect, German citizen Christian Brückner, was announced to have been linked to the case. Brückner is a convicted rapist and child sex abuser, and as of 2022 is in jail for raping a woman in the same area that Madeleine went missing.

The British government estimates that the case has cost more than ten million pounds. Madeleine McCann remains a missing person.

———————————

LAUREEN RAHN

Laureen Rahn was a student at Parkside Junior High School and lived with her mother, Judith Rahn, in Manchester, New Hampshire. Rahn was described by family as happy and outgoing but had starting hanging out alone on the streets, smoking marijuana, drinking alcohol, and reportedly talking about running away from home.

On April 26, 1980, Rahn was left alone in the apartment when Judith went out of town to watch her boyfriend's tennis match. Rahn was on spring break from school and usually went with her mother to the tennis games but had asked to stay home. Rahn's family members checked on her during the day, and she had been seen hanging out at a convenience store on the block. That night Rahn invited a female friend and a male friend to drink alcohol at her apartment.

At 12:30 a.m. on April 27, Rahn and her male friend heard voices in the apartment building's hallway, and he left through the back door, assuming the voice was Rahn's mother, to avoid getting in trouble. The male friend told investigators he heard Rahn lock the door behind him, and another neighbor confirmed hearing voices in the hallway at that time. At around 1:15 a.m., Judith returned home with her boyfriend and found that the lightbulbs on all of the floors of the apartment building had been unscrewed and the hallways were pitch-black. When they arrived home, Judith noticed the front door was unlocked and saw a person in Laureen's bed, and assumed it was Laureen. Judith's boyfriend found that the back door was open, and when Judith approached Laureen's bed to ask her why it was open, she realized that the girl in the bed was Laureen's friend, who claimed Laureen had gone to sleep on the couch. After calling family members to see if Laureen was at their house, Judith and her boyfriend went to search the neighborhood. At 3:45 a.m., Judith reported her daughter missing to the officer in a nearby police car.

Police initially believed Rahn had run away, but when she did not return, they began to believe foul play was involved. A bus company employee told authorities he sold a ticket to a girl who matched Rahn's description, and a driver later identified Rahn as a girl he dropped off in Boston. In October

1980, Judith found that she had been charged for three phone calls in California, although she did not have relatives there; the calls came from two motels in Santa Monica and Santa Ana, the latter of which was referred to as a teen sexual assistance hotline. Karole Jensen, an investigator for Wings for Children, traveled to California and found that one of the motels the phone calls were made from was suspected to be a host for the production of child pornography, but Rahn was never officially linked to the motel.

For several years after Rahn disappeared, family members and friends received strange phone calls. Judith received calls for several years, always around 3:45 a.m. and increasing around Christmastime, and she believed it was Rahn who made the calls. Rahn's aunt also received a call from a young girl who asked for her cousin Mike, a nickname only Rahn used. In 1986, a childhood friend of Rahn's received a call from someone claiming to be "Laurie," and when his mother answered, the girl stated that she was his former girlfriend; Rahn had dated him when they were twelve years old.

There have also been alleged sightings in Boston by Rahn's aunt, and a witness claimed to see a sex worker in Anchorage, Alaska, who matched Rahn's description. Although he was never considered a suspect, the male friend who last saw Rahn alive died by suicide in 1985.

DANNETTE AND JEANNETTE MILLBROOK

Dannette and Jeannette Millbrook were teenage fraternal twins who went missing in 1990. The Millbrook twins were students at Lucy Laney High School in Augusta, Georgia, and had no history of getting involved in trouble, sans one time when they were being bullied at the bus stop.

On March 18, 1990, Dannette and Jeannette walked to a nearby Church's Chicken restaurant for lunch and told their mother, upon their return, that a van had followed them for a portion of their walk back home. Later that day, the girls walked to their godfather's house to ask for money to take the bus to school. The twins then walked to their cousin's house and then their sister's, asking both of them to walk them home, but they declined. Their final stop was a local gas station, where the Millbrook twins bought snacks from the clerk, Gloria, who stated she saw nothing out of the ordinary about their behavior, and who was the last person to see Dannette and Jeannette. Although neither girl had a history of running away, the family was told to wait twenty-four hours before reporting them missing.

The original 1990 investigation was closed within a year, and little is known about it, due to the original police file being lost. The initial investigation was not thorough, with police often misspelling "Millbrook" or Jeannette's middle name in case files, causing many online missing persons databases to list the incorrect name today. After persistence from the Millbrook family, the case was officially reopened in 2013 by the Richmond County Sheriff's Office.

In 1993, remains of an unidentified Black woman were found in nearby Aiken County, which the Millbrook family believes could be Jeannette, based on facial reconstructions. The DNA of the Jane Doe has yet to be compared to the Millbrook's familial DNA, and police told the family they ruled out the twins as a possible match.

Some internet sleuths believe the Millbrook twins could have been victims of serial killer Joseph Patrick Washington, who lived in Augusta at the time of their disappearance. Washington would have had to pass the gas station where the Millbrook girls were last seen in order to go to work. Washington died in prison in 1999, before any conclusive evidence could be found tying him to the girls' disappearance.

BEN NEEDHAM

Ben Needham was an English baby who disappeared in Kos, a Greek island, while visiting his grandparents with his parents. Needham was born on October 29, 1989, in Boston, Lincolnshire, to Kerry Needham and Simon Ward.

Ben and his family were staying in his mother's parents' farmhouse in Kos when he mysteriously disappeared in 1991, when he was twenty-one months old. Ben had been playing around his grandparents' farmhouse when his family realized he had disappeared, at around 2:30 p.m. on July 24, 1991. The family searched the area and assumed he had either wandered off or been taken on a moped with his uncle Stephen. The Needhams called the police to report him missing, but the police began to suspect the family, which distracted them from reporting the missing child to nearby ports and airports. No trace of Ben was located by either Greek or British police. They believe that he died due to an accident relating to "heavy machinery," perhaps involving a nearby construction worker who allegedly admitted to killing Ben accidently and burying his body to hide the evidence. This construction worker died in 2015 and is not believed to be a suspect by police. Experts have continued to search and test soil in the area in hopes of finding any evidence of Ben, to no avail.

There have been hundreds of potential sightings of Ben that seem to encourage the theory that Ben was sold into adoption, was kidnapped, or fell victim to human trafficking. In 1995, a private investigator found a boy around six years old whom he believed could be Ben, but determined through his birth certificate that he was not Ben. In 2015, a man came forward believing that he may be Ben, but police confirmed it was not he. In July 2021, a newspaper from Corfu, Greece, reported that in 1991 a boy had been discovered by a teenage girl, who took him to her workplace to ask families if they recognized him.

Two other witnesses came forward saying they saw the boy, who was only wearing a white T-shirt. Another witness said the boy looked to be around one or two years old and extremely distraught; after seeing a picture of Ben in the news, she believed that boy was the same person she had seen in Corfu. The teenager who found him apparently never returned to work and kept the child and raised him herself. According to those witnesses, the boy speaks Greek and continues to live in the area. Ben's mother, Kerry, reached out to the owner of the teenager's place of work for information, but he passed away two days after her reaching out to him. South Yorkshire police believe that Ben passed away, but Ben's mother has continued to search for him and believes that he is alive.

NATALEE HOLLOWAY

Natalee Holloway was an American teenager who mysteriously disappeared in 2005 while on a high school graduation trip in Aruba. Holloway graduated from Mountain Brook High School in Birmingham, Alabama, in May 2005, and planned to attend the University of Alabama in the fall.

On May 26, 2005, Holloway, along with 124 other Mountain Brook graduates, arrived in Aruba for an unofficial graduation trip with seven chaperones; the chaperones were only supposed to check in once a day. The group was staying in a Holiday Inn, and the students were excessively drinking and partying, so much so that the hotel banned the school from staying there the following year. Friends of Holloway stated to investigators that Holloway was drinking every day and didn't show up to the group breakfast twice during the trip.

Holloway was last seen on May 30, 2005, at approximately 1:30 a.m.; classmates recall she was leaving the Oranjestad nightclub Carlos 'n Charlie's with seventeen-year-old Joran van der Sloot, a Dutch student at the International School of Aruba, and Surinamese brothers Deepak Kalpoe (twenty-one) and Satish Kalpoe (eighteen). Holloway was scheduled to fly back to the United States that day, but did not return to the airport, and her luggage and passport were found in her hotel room. Van der Sloot told authorities that they dropped off Holloway at her hotel at around 2:00 a.m., and that he saw a man approach Holloway as they were driving away. Holloway's mother and stepfather flew to Aruba to help law enforcement

search for their daughter. On June 5, two security guards were arrested on suspicion of kidnapping and murder but were released about a week later without being charged.

Van der Sloot and the Kalpoe brothers were arrested on June 9 on suspicion of kidnapping and killing Holloway, and several other potential accomplices were arrested, but then released. Van der Sloot and the Kalpoes changed their stories several times while they were detained. Searches in several locations came up with no evidence. In 2007, the Dutch National Police took over the case. Over the course of several years, van der Sloot told journalists different stories about Holloway: that he left her at the beach, that Holloway had died of alcohol poisoning and he disposed of the body, that he had sold Holloway into sexual slavery (which he stated to Fox News), and that his father had paid off police officers to hide the fact that she had been taken to Venezuela (the latter of which he retracted).

In 2010, van der Sloot attempted to extort the Holloway family for $25,000 in exchange for information about the location of Holloway's body. The information he gave her mother was false, and van der Sloot was indicted for extortion and wire fraud by the Court of Northern Alabama.

On May 30, 2010 (the fifth anniversary of Holloway's disappearance), Stephany Flores Ramírez was found dead in a hotel room registered under van der Sloot's name in Lima, Peru. Van der Sloot confessed to murdering Ramírez when she found information on his laptop about Holloway's disappearance. In 2012, van der Sloot was sentenced to twenty-eight years in prison for the murder of Ramírez. Holloway was declared legally dead in 2012.

RONALD HENRY TAMMEN JR.

Ronald Tammen Jr.'s is another of those cases where someone walks out into the night and simply vanishes. He was a college student at Miami University in Oxford, Ohio. On the night of April 19, 1953, he had been in his dorm room, and had requested new bedsheets at 8:00 p.m., because someone had put a dead fish in his bed as a joke (a pretty awful college prank!). Sometime during the next hour or so, he heard a disturbing sound outside and left to investigate what it was.

When his roommate came back at about 10:00 p.m. and found Tammen gone, he didn't think anything of it—until Tammen didn't return the following day.

All of Tammen's important personal possessions were still in the room: clothing, wallet, car keys, ID, and so on. His car was still in its parking spot, with his fiddle in the backseat. Clearly, he was not intending to be gone very long, and was not trying to secretly sneak away. But police couldn't find any evidence that he was kidnapped either. He was a strong, athletic guy, and if someone were trying to take him against his will, he definitely would have fought back, and would probably cause some damage. It seems he went out for some reason, not expecting to be gone long, and then something happened to convince him not to come back.

A woman about twenty miles away said a young man came to her door at about 11:00 p.m. the night of Tammen's disappearance and asked her what town he was in. He also asked for directions to a bus stop, which she offered, and then he left. She said he was dirty and messy, and seemed confused, and he was not wearing a coat or hat, even though the night was cold. It could have been Tammen, but his own family doesn't think it was. And how would he have gotten that far away in only an hour, unless he was taken there? Also, there was no bus service that night, so he wouldn't have gotten much farther.

A few other details were weird. Exactly five months before his disappearance, Tammen went to the coroner's office in Hamilton, about ten miles away, to have his blood typed (he ended up being O positive). The coroner said that no one had ever asked him to do this before. And furthermore, why did Tammen bother to go all that way, when he could have easily done it in Oxford? The university even had a hospital.

One researcher who has studied the case believes something stranger may have happened. She claims that one of Tammen's professors worked for the CIA, and that the agency secretly recruited him that night. If so, he disappeared into a world of espionage, and couldn't come back to his old life. It seems that the FBI only got rid of Tammen's fingerprint records in 2002, and their own regulations forbid them from getting rid of these until a person has been dead for seven years. Did Tammen live on in secret for forty years? If so, his family has a right to know.

TAMMY LYNN LEPPERT

Tammy Lynn Leppert was an American former child actress, model, and beauty queen who went missing in Florida when she was eighteen.

Leppert was born in Florida in 1965 and began modeling and doing beauty pageants at four years old. She competed in around 300 beauty pageants and won 280 crowns, and was on the cover of *CoverGirl* magazine in October 1978. She had an uncredited role in *Scarface* and had other minor roles in *Little Darlings* and *Spring Break.* Shortly before her disappearance, Leppert went to a party alone, after which her friends and family stated she had returned as "a different person." While filming *Scarface,* Leppert returned home after four days of filming; according to Leppert's mother, Tammy was scared of being murdered and spent seventy-two hours in a medical center but was released after they didn't find any signs of drugs or alcohol abuse.

On July 6, 1983, Leppert was last seen in Cocoa Beach, Florida, and it was speculated that she may have been three months pregnant. A friend of Leppert's told investigators that he had an argument with her while driving her from Rockledge, and he left her in a parking lot. Her friend was most likely to be the last person to see her alive, and while her mother claimed Leppert was afraid of him, he is not considered a suspect.

Investigators looked into several theories in Leppert's disappearance. One theory was that Leppert was a victim of serial killer Christopher Wilder, also known as the Beauty Queen Killer, who killed at least eight young women before he was killed by police in 1984. While Wilder is still a viable suspect, he did not start his killing spree until a year after Leppert disappeared. Convicted kidnapper and rapist John Crutchley, who is also suspected of killing up to thirty women, is also another person of interest.

Tammy Lynn Leppert is still considered a missing person.

BRIAN SHAFFER

Brian Shaffer was an Ohio State University medical student who went missing in 2006. After graduating from Ohio State with a degree in microbiology, Shaffer enrolled in the Ohio State College of Medicine in 2004.

On March 31, 2006, Shaffer went to dinner with his father, Randy Shaffer, to celebrate the beginning of spring break. Shaffer's father later told authorities that Shaffer seemed exhausted and worried about going out with his friend, Clint Florence. Shaffer met Florence at a Columbus bar, the Ugly Tuna Saloona, at the South Campus Gateway complex on High Street at 9:00 p.m. While there, Shaffer spoke to his girlfriend, Alexis Waggoner, on the phone before he and Florence bar-hopped, heading toward the Arena District. Sometime after midnight, Shaffer and Florence got a ride from Meredith Reed, a friend of Florence's, who drove them back to the Ugly Tuna Saloona.

After returning to the bar, Shaffer separated from Reed and Florence. The pair were unable to reach him by phone and waited outside the bar for him when it closed at 2:00 a.m. Florence and Reed left the area, assuming Shaffer had walked back to his apartment. Neither Waggoner nor Shaffer's father was able to reach him that weekend.

Shaffer was reported missing when he didn't show up to the flight he was scheduled to take with Waggoner to Miami. Authorities reviewed the security footage from the Ugly Tuna Saloona, where Shaffer was seen talking to two young women outside the bar at 1:55 a.m. After saying good-bye to the two women, Shaffer was seen walking off camera toward the bar. This was the last time Shaffer was seen alive. Police searched the area extensively but found nothing; Shaffer's apartment appeared normal, and his car was still parked outside his apartment building.

No prominent theory pointed toward Shaffer being a victim of foul play, deliberately disappearing, or getting into an accident. For a long time after Shaffer's disappearance, Waggoner would call Shaffer's phone before going to bed; it always went to voicemail, but one night it rang three times, with a ping being detected in Hilliard, Ohio. Shaffer's father passed away in September 2008, and a signature on his online obituary read, "To Dad, love Brian," but was found to be a hoax. Everyone who saw Shaffer took a lie detector test and passed, but Florence refused. Waggoner and private investigators believe that Florence knows more than he let on.

KRISTIN SMART

Kristin Smart was born in West Germany in 1977 to two American military personnel. When she was a child, the family moved to Stockton, California. In 1996, after graduating from high school, Smart enrolled in California Polytechnic State University, San Luis Obispo (Cal Poly).

On May 25, 1996, Smart's friend dropped her off at a birthday party at a fraternity house; it is believed she didn't know anyone at the party. At around 2:00 a.m., students Cheryl Anderson and Tim Davis found Smart passed out on a neighbor's lawn after leaving the party. Anderson, Davis, and another student, Paul Flores, helped walk Smart back to her dormitory. Davis left the group to drive back to his off-campus housing, and Anderson left Smart with Flores to go to Sierra Madre Hall. Flores stated to police that he walked Kristin as far as Santa Lucia Hall, where he lived, and left her to walk to the Muir Hall dorm alone. This was the last confirmed sighting of Smart. At the time of her disappearance, Smart did not have cash or credit cards on her.

Despite the Smart family calling police, University police were slow in reporting her as a missing person because they believed Smart had gone on an unannounced vacation. Volunteers searched the area, using horses and ground-penetrating radar devices. For a short time, Scott Peterson, convicted of killing his wife, Laci, in 2003, was believed to have been involved in Smart's disappearance, due to him going to Cal Poly at the time; however, nothing tied him to Smart, and he was ruled out as a suspect.

In 2016, investigators from the San Luis Obispo County Sheriff's Office led cadaver dogs from the FBI to a part of the Cal Poly campus, where items were found in three dig sites and are currently under investigation.

While Smart's body has never been recovered, Paul Flores and his father, Ruben, were charged with murder and accessory, respectively, in April 2021, and are on trial in Monterey County, after investigators found date-rape drugs and videos of Flores raping young women. Further, a tenant at the former home of Paul Flores found an earring that may have belonged to Smart, but it was lost in police custody.

Smart's disappearance and the slow response by campus police resulted in the California State Legislature signing into effect a new law called the Kristin Smart Campus Security Act, which requires all public colleges and publicly funded educational institutions in California to have agreements with local law enforcement about reporting cases involving violence against students, which includes those who are missing.

CHAPTER 7
MODERN-DAY MYSTERIES

MOST OF US HAVE SMARTPHONES that track our every movement. There are security cameras everywhere you look. Businesses won't go without them, and now even many homes have cameras installed to ensure that no intruders can enter undetected. With the amount of surveillance that's now woven into our daily lives, you would think that it would be impossible to vanish without someone or something recording where you went. And yet hundreds of thousands of people worldwide go missing every year. In the United States, more than 2,000 people are reported missing every day. This chapter includes some of the most confounding mysteries of modern-day adults who managed to disappear from a world that makes it nearly impossible to be lost.

SEAN FLYNN AND
DANA STONE

Sean Flynn and Dana Stone were photojournalists who were captured while on an assignment in Cambodia. Sean Flynn was the child of Australian-American actor Errol Flynn and French-American actress Lili Damita. Flynn was also an actor prior to becoming a freelance photojournalist in the 1960s, when he became known for high-risk photos during the Vietnam War. Flynn worked for CBS News, *Paris Match,* Time Life, and United Press International. Dana Stone was also known as a high-risk photojournalist who worked for United Press International, the Associated Press, and CBS News.

Flynn and Stone often worked together, and in April 1970, the pair were called to Cambodia to record North Vietnamese advances. While in Phnom Penh, Flynn and Stone decided to take motorcycles to a government-sponsored press conference in Saigon, while the other reporters chose to travel in a limousine. Fellow reporter Steve Bell stated that Flynn and Stone had been near a makeshift checkpoint along Highway 1 that was believed to be created by Viet Cong members. According to film footage and witness statements, it is believed that Flynn and Stone approached the checkpoint and were taken to a tree line by members of the Viet Cong, never to be seen again. The last photo of Flynn and Stone was taken by Bell shortly before their disappearance.

The same day that Flynn and Stone disappeared, four other journalists from France and Japan were also captured by the Viet Cong in Cambodia. By June of that year, twenty-five photojournalists had been captured. Out of the twenty-five captured, three were killed, a handful returned home, and the rest are missing. Flynn and Stone are among the missing, and their bodies have never been recovered. Although it is confirmed that the two men were captured by Viet Cong guerillas at the checkpoint, their fate is unknown. However, it is believed that they were killed by members of the Khmer Rouge. Flynn's mother, Lili Damita, searched for her son for over ten years, and had him declared legally dead in 1984. Stone's brother, John Thomas Stone, joined the US Army in 1971 in order to find out the fate of Stone, but died in 2006 while serving as a medic for the Vermont National Guard.

While their fate is unknown, their disappearance has sparked many books, films, and other creations, including Perry Deane Young's memoir, *Two of the Missing,* the 1991 film *Danger on the Edge of Town,* the Clash song "Sean Flynn," the 2011 film *The Road to Freedom,* and a character in Francis Ford Coppola's *Apocalypse Now* who is based on Flynn.

BRUCE CAMPBELL SR.

Bruce Campbell Sr. and his wife, Mabelita, had made a very long drive from Massachusetts to Illinois to visit their son, Bruce Jr., their son's wife, and their new grandchild. They arrived on April 13, 1959.

Long drives like that can really take a toll, and Bruce Sr. was definitely exhausted and not feeling well. Their son didn't have room for them at his home, so he arranged for them to stay at the nearby Sandman Motel, where Bruce Sr. rested. But his son noticed his dad was behaving strangely, even acting paranoid. A doctor came to visit him in the motel room and prescribed some sleeping pills for him, but he seemed out of it in more ways than one.

The following night, his wife remembered him being restless and acting paranoid once again. Bruce Sr. woke her up twice before 1:00 a.m. to ask if the car door was locked. She assured him it was, and told him to go back to sleep. She woke up again at about 2:15 a.m. to see that she was alone. She got up in a hurry and searched the room. All of her husband's belongings were there, including his glasses, keys, and wallet. The only things not there were the green pajamas he'd worn to bed, so he must have left the room still wearing them. Their room opened up directly to the parking lot, but she saw that their car was still there, and locked just as she'd assured him it was.

She went to the desk clerk, who told her he had not seen anyone walk by. She called the police, and they came out to search the area, but they couldn't find

Bruce Sr. anywhere. The following day, they started a much wider search, eventually enlisting the help of hundreds of volunteers, but they came up empty. As is so often the case with these strange stories, Bruce Sr. just seemed to vanish off the face of the earth. But how far could a fifty-seven-year-old man wearing only pajamas have actually gone? He was also tall (over six feet, making him recognizable) and had a slight limp, so it seems unlikely that he could have wandered too far.

There were a few clues: one farmer not too far away claimed to have been woken up by shouting that same night, though police didn't find anything when investigating. It seemed like he may have been picked up by a driver and taken somewhere (as in, kidnapped), but where? Why did he act nervous and paranoid on the night he vanished, like he knew someone was coming for him? The Campbells had a happy marriage and no financial troubles or other worries; Bruce Sr. had never acted this way before. Neither Mabelita nor Bruce Jr. could come up with any reasons as to why his behavior changed, or why he just seemingly wandered off, never to be seen again. No trace of Bruce Campbell Sr. has ever been found.

ASHA KREIMER

Unlike stories of people wandering off into the woods or disappearing at night, poor Asha Kreimer somehow disappeared in the middle of the day, and in a busy area, where dozens of people should have seen her but didn't. Even stranger is that before her disappearance, Kreimer had started behaving very strangely, and no one really knew why. She was originally from Australia, but around the time of the incident was living with her boyfriend, Jamai Gayle, in Albion, California, a coastal town several hours north of San Francisco. The couple was happy and everything was fine, according to friends who knew them. But in September 2015, things became disturbing.

Kreimer started to act very strangely. She would shout at random times, go into what seemed like trances, and often refuse to eat for days at a time.

Gayle was very worried, because this was completely unlike Asha, so he took her to a mental health facility. Though Kreimer had no history of mental illness, the doctor suggested that she might be suffering from bipolar disorder and might have had some kind of breakdown due to an unknown source of stress. But she was not believed to be a danger to herself, and the doctor let her go back with Gayle. Unfortunately, her behavior only got worse.

Sally Scales, a friend, was visiting from Australia, and she also witnessed these odd behaviors. It made no sense to her either, because Kreimer had never acted this way before. Gayle decided that a visit to his mom down in San Francisco might be a great way to get out of the house and change of scenery. They drove down the coast to a town called Flumeville, where the trio stopped at a café for breakfast.

Scales at one point went to the restroom, and a minute later, Kreimer also said that she was going. Scales returned to the table, but she hadn't seen Kreimer go into the restroom, even though Gayle saw her walk that way. They waited for a bit, but soon, it was obvious that Asha wasn't there. It was the last time either of them would see her. She'd left her shoes at the table, and her bag with her wallet, ID, and money. No one recalled seeing her leave the café, and no one outside saw her. The police did a search, but found nothing.

Searchers did find Asha's jacket at a lighthouse nearby, and at first, they feared she might have killed herself by jumping off a cliff into the ocean. But there were no signs that she'd gone to the cliff, and in any case, no one saw anything. Someone claimed they saw her at the beach later that afternoon, but it couldn't be proven. Another said they were sure they saw her in a supermarket a few days later, but again, they had no proof. It turned out that she'd left her cell phone in some bushes near her home, and a couple of messages were deleted off it the day she went missing. This was definitely suspicious, but didn't yield any clues.

What's disturbing about this case is the huge change in Asha's personality not long before her disappearance. It may well have been a mental health issue, and that may have led to her running away, but how was she able to vanish from a café in broad daylight without being seen? Why did no one see her leave the café or wander around town? The case remains a mystery.

WILL CIERZAN

Will Cierzan told his wife, Linda, that he was cooking dinner and that it would be ready soon. He had been at home on January 26, 2017, watching golf on TV with his nephew, who left afterward.

He seemed to be in a great mood, and she was looking forward to coming home and having a nice meal. But when Linda arrived home before 7:00 p.m., there was no sign of her husband. Dinner was done, the oven was turned off, his coat and wallet with money were there, and the dog was in the house, but Will wasn't. And no one has seen him since.

Police investigators came to their home and searched. They found traces of blood that matched Will's, and a surveillance camera from a neighbor's home showed that at some point, a white SUV backed up into the driveway at around 5:00 p.m., but it left a few minutes later, and Will was not in the footage. It seems that Will was attacked and kidnapped, and removed from his house without anyone seeing or hearing anything. Who did it?

The obvious first choice of suspects was his nephew, who was there while they watched golf that afternoon. And for a while, he was a person of interest to the police. But he cooperated fully with them, and wasn't charged with anything. Also, there didn't seem to have been any record of him and Will not getting along. If he did it, why? Nothing was stolen from the house, so it must have been a personal grudge. But again, the police never arrested the nephew.

A skull and other remains have since been found in the area, but tests showed they weren't Will's, so he's still missing. It doesn't seem likely that Will left his house willingly. The blood and the fact that his money was still in the house prove that. It also didn't seem like it was a robbery. Someone had him marked as a target and waited for the nephew to leave before moving in and taking him. But who and why? And how was this kidnapper able to get Will out of the house in broad daylight with no one seeing? Who was in the SUV, and why did it park for a few minutes at Will's home before leaving? Was he snuck out a back door? There are so many questions about this case, and for now, the answers are still out there.

MARION BARTER

Marion Barter was a schoolteacher who lived on the northeast coast of Australia, an area called the "Gold Coast." She seemed to be content enough, teaching and living a regular life. But in her personal life, things were not so good. She had been married three times, and in the mid-1990s, the third marriage ended. Undoubtedly, she was very unhappy and feeling the need for change, but what happened next would leave her friends baffled. In 1997, she decided to do something impulsive. She sold her home, took some of the money, and went on a vacation to Europe, which for her was on the other side of the world. It may have been a bit out of the blue, but considering what she'd been going through, the move was understandable. She left in June and, for a while, sent postcards and gifts to friends and family back in Australia.

This was normal enough, but on August 1, things changed. Her daughter, Sally Leydon, received a message on her answering machine. It was her mom, calling to tell her that she was in the town of Tunbridge Wells in southern England. Barter was calling from a pay phone, and had to keep adding coins to it, since it would have been very expensive to call that far. She explained that she was having tea with some older women and was having a great time. But she started to run out of coins, so she had to end the call. She said, "I'll call you back," and hung up. No one ever heard from her again.

Her daughter thought she was definitely calling from England, because there was a delay and an echo in Marion's voice, which indicated the call was coming from a long distance. But so many questions came up. Why had she gone off to Europe on such a whim? Why did she call that day? Who were the women she was having tea with? Why did she say she would call back, but never did? Then, the mystery deepened.

In October, large amounts of money were withdrawn from Barter's bank account...from locations in Queensland, Australia. Leydon also learned that less than a day after talking to her mother on the phone, Marion's passport was marked as returning to Australia via the city of Brisbane on the northeast coast. Was her mother back in the country in secret? Had she lied about being in England after all? The police would only tell her daughter that Barter was alive, but didn't want to be contacted, which made no sense at all.

Amazingly, Leydon and Marion's father spent years trying to figure out what happened. In 2009, they learned that Marion had legally changed her name in May 1997, right before her supposed trip. She had planned a return trip for August 2, but claimed that she lived in the small European country of Luxembourg, and was only passing through Australia. On August 13, her medical information was used in the Gold Coast area, and other records showed she might never have left Australia at all. It was completely baffling that these various government agencies couldn't find her. And they still can't.

Leydon did receive a mysterious Facebook message in 2013 that claimed Marion was alive, but that her daughter would never see her again. She thinks her mother was kidnapped, but as of 2022, there is no more information. Somehow Marion Barter slipped through the cracks of modern society, and no one can find her.

LARS MITTANK

He shouldn't have gotten into a fight, but it was about football, and it seemed important at the time. Lars Mittank was a German man who was vacationing with some friends at a resort called Golden Sands in Bulgaria in July 2014. It was a popular place for young adults and college students from both Germany and England, but on July 6, Lars got into a fight with some other tourists over their favorite football teams (football, aka soccer, is hugely popular in much of the world outside of the United States).

This argument led to a fistfight, and during the fight, Mittank got punched in the ear. The blow was so hard that it damaged his eardrum. He visited a doctor who told him not to fly until it had healed up. He eventually recommended that Mittank stay in a hospital, where the injury could be further checked out.

Lars's friends wanted to stay with him, but he told them he was fine and that they should go on home. Once he was on his own, he checked into a local hotel, but almost immediately, he started acting strangely. Cameras showed him acting oddly, and witnesses said he seemed paranoid and scared of something. He ended up spending only one night in the hotel, but while he was there, he phoned his mother and told her that four men were trying to kill him, and that he wanted her to cancel his credit cards. The following day, he went back to the doctor, who reported that Mittank jumped up and ran away as soon as he arrived. Not long after that, Lars was at the airport, even though he'd been advised not to fly yet.

Security camera footage showed him entering the airport with his luggage and seeming to act normal, but soon, the same camera recorded him running back out, this time without his luggage. Other cameras caught him running across the terminal, and eventually climbing over a fence and taking off into a field. Despite a widespread search, no one has seen him since. His family can't explain why Lars acted the way he did, why he thought someone was after him, or why he would and could just disappear. He had no history of mental or psychological issues. He was just a regular young man having a vacation with his friends.

Could that punch to his ear have damaged his brain somehow? It seems very unlikely, but the fact that he only began to act oddly after the fight could mean that's the case. But even if something had happened to him, how was it possible that he just vanished completely? Was someone really after him? Did he see them at the airport? If so, who were they? And why didn't they chase him?

It seems unlikely that it would have been the guys he got into a fight with over football, but no one has come up with any better explanations. Mittank ran away from something he believed was threatening him, and has never been seen since.

GLEN STEWART GODWIN

Glen Stewart Godwin is an American convicted murderer and fugitive who was on the FBI Top Ten Most Wanted Fugitives list for twenty years. In 1980, Godwin was living in Palm Springs, California, as a self-employed construction worker, mechanic, and salesman with no known criminal history. Godwin and his roommate, Frank Soto Jr., planned to rob Kim Robert LeValley, a pilot and drug dealer. Godwin and Soto lured LeValley to their condo, where Godwin stabbed him. The pair loaded LeValley into a truck and attempted to blow up the evidence in the desert. On August 3, Eagle Mountain residents found a blown-up truck with human remains in it, which led police to Godwin and Soto. Soto testified against Godwin, and they were both sentenced to twenty-five years in prison in 1983.

In 1987, Godwin tried to escape the Deuel Vocational Institute but was moved to the maximum-security Folsom State Prison. Police believe Godwin's wife, Shelly, and his former cellmate, Lorenz Karlic, helped smuggle a hacksaw and other tools into his cell on June 5, 1987. Godwin cut a hole through the fence wire and escaped through a storm drain that led to the American River. An accomplice (suspected to be his wife or Karlic) left a raft, which Godwin used to follow painted rocks down the river. Karlic and Shelly were arrested in 1987 and 1990, respectively.

Godwin fled to Mexico, where he participated in the illegal drug trade and was arrested for drug trafficking in Puerto Vallarta in 1991. While American law enforcement were trying to get Godwin extradited, he allegedly killed a member of a Mexican drug cartel while in prison. This delayed his extradition, giving Godwin time to escape again in September 1991. Godwin is believed to be involved in the drug trade in Latin America and considered to be armed and extremely dangerous, as well as a flight risk.

SUKUMARA KURUP

Sukumara Kurup, or Sukumara Pillai, is a fugitive from justice and is one of the most wanted criminals in the state of Kerala, India. He has become infamous for being India's longest-wanted criminal.

Born in 1946 in Cheriyanad, Kurup had a short-lived career in the Air Force before legally changing his name and working as an executive for a marine petroleum company in Abu Dhabi. In 1984, Kurup forcefully intoxicated, poisoned, and murdered a man named Chacko with the help of his brother-in-law Bhaskara Pillai, his driver, Ponnappan, and his aide, Shahu. Allegedly, Kurup murdered Chacko because he had a striking resemblance to him and he wanted to fake his own death to claim the insurance money. It is believed that Kurup fled, while his driver and brother-in-law were sentenced to life in prison, and his aide made a deal with police.

Kurup has not been heard from since 1984. He is wanted for murder, criminal conspiracy, causing the disappearance of evidence, intentional omission, and dishonest misappropriation of property possessed by a deceased person.

The case garnered media attention in the 2000s due to Kurup lookalikes in various parts of the world. After closing investigations after twelve years of searching, investigators believe that due to his seventy-two-hour head start, Kurup successfully fled the country with help from political allies. However, some believe that Kurup stayed in India under a pseudonym, Joshi, and may have passed away in the 1990s due to cardiac issues. Former DGP Alexander Jacob revealed in 2021 that police had apprehended Kurup but failed to identify him in his disguise and let him go. Despite whatever fate Kurup found, his legacy is remembered in India, and his status as an urban legend has sparked several film adaptations.

SUSAN POWELL

Susan Powell went missing on December 6, 2009, in West Valley, Utah. That morning, Susan and her two sons, Charlie and Braden, went to church services and visited with a neighbor until 5:00 p.m. On December 7, Susan, her sons, and her husband, Joshua Powell, were reported missing, and, after failing to reach the family, police entered their home and did not find them there—and there was a strange wet spot on the couch. Police found Susan's purse, wallet, and ID inside the house.

At around 5:00 p.m. on December 7, Joshua and his sons returned to the house, claiming that he had left Susan alone in the house around midnight to go on a camping trip with his children. However, police failed to find any evidence that they had been at the campsite, and it was noted that Utah was experiencing blizzard conditions, so it would be unlikely that anyone would go camping.

Investigators found traces of Susan's blood on the floor of the house and a life insurance policy on Susan for over a million dollars. They also found that Susan had handwritten a letter in her will, stating that there was turmoil in the marriage and she feared for her life. It was revealed that Joshua had filed for bankruptcy in 2007. It was also revealed that Joshua's father, Steven, had an infatuation with Susan when the couple lived in his home and often secretly recorded her, stole her undergarments, and read her journals. After Steven confessed his feelings for Susan, she moved across state lines with Joshua and her children and felt uncomfortable that Joshua stayed in contact with his family.

After Susan's disappearance, Joshua took financial action that was deemed suspicious by police, including taking his sons out of daycare and liquidating Susan's retirement accounts. When interviewed by police, the elder son, Charlie, confirmed that the family had taken a camping trip with Susan but that she did not return with them. Both Charlie and Braden expressed to teachers that their mom was dead and had been hidden in the trunk of Joshua's car. Joshua became uncooperative in the investigation, retained an attorney, and moved his sons in with Steven before becoming a person of interest in Susan's disappearance.

Joshua's family began a website dedicated to Susan, claiming that Susan's family was making Joshua a victim of a smear campaign, alleging Susan abandoned her family due to mental illness and even that she and Steven Koecher, another person from the area that went missing the same week as Susan, had eloped in Brazil. These claims are believed to have been written by Joshua and Steven.

In 2010, investigators uncovered over 4,000 images of Susan that Steven had taken without her knowledge and a truck formerly owned by Joshua's brother, Michael. Sniffer dogs found the scent of a decomposed body in the truck's bed. On September 22, 2011, Steven was arrested for voyeurism and child pornography, which caused Susan's parents to file for and win custody of Charlie and Braden.

On February 5, 2012, Joshua killed both his sons and himself in a murder-suicide arson. A year later, Joshua's brother, Michael, died by suicide, and Steven Powell passed away after being released from prison. Susan's case remains closed, but investigators believe that Joshua, with the help of his father and brother, killed Susan.

JOHN RUFFO

John Ruffo is an American white-collar criminal and fugitive who disappeared in 1998. Ruffo earned a computer science degree from New York University and worked at United Computer Systems LLC before creating his own firm, Consolidated Computer Services (CCS). Former Philip Morris USA executive Edward J. Reiners approached Ruffo in 1992 with a scheme to solicit several banks under the guise of raising funds for a fictitious project for Philip Morris. Ruffo and Reiners forged documents and had banks sign NDAs to prevent them from speaking with Philip Morris directly.

In 1996, the Long-Term Credit Bank of Japan found an irregularity on one of the forged documents and contacted both Philip Morris and the FBI. The FBI set up a sting operation and arrested Reiners on March 19, 1996, and issued an arrest warrant for Ruffo. The scheme is believed to have generated over $350 million. Ruffo was considered a flight risk, and his initial bail was set at $10 million. Nearly all of Ruffo's assets and accounts were frozen, and his immediate family put up their homes as collateral in order to secure the pretrial release of Ruffo. Ruffo was found guilty on 150 counts of bank fraud, money laundering, wire fraud, and conspiracy; he was sentenced to seventeen years in prison.

Ruffo failed to turn himself over to the US Marshals Service in November 1998 and was spotted on CCTV cameras taking money out of an ATM. Ruffo's car was found abandoned at John F. Kennedy International Airport by the FBI. In early 1999, the homes of Ruffo's wife, mother, mother-in-law, and other family members were seized by the government as bond collateral, making them all homeless.

In April 2001, Ruffo was sighted in Duncan, Oklahoma, while attempting to open a bank account to receive $250 million from Nigerian wire transfers, but when authorities came to apprehend him, he had already left town. In 2016, Ruffo's cousin believed he spotted Ruffo in the crowd of a Los Angeles Dodgers game, but it was later proved that the man was not Ruffo. Ruffo is still at large and is on the US Marshals 15 Most Wanted Fugitives list.

ROBERT FISHER

Robert Fisher, also known as Bobby Fisher, is an American fugitive who was on the FBI Ten Most Wanted Fugitive list for nine years and is still at large. Fisher was born in 1961 and moved to Arizona at age fifteen with his father and sisters after his parents divorced in 1976. He enlisted in the US Navy but failed in his attempts to become a part of the SEALs. He briefly worked as a firefighter in California, but was forced to retire due to a back injury. He then moved his family back to Arizona, where he worked a variety of jobs: surgical catheter technician, respiratory therapist, weed sprayer, and surgical technician at a Mayo Clinic.

Fisher married Mary Cooper in 1987 and was described as cruel, distant, and controlling of his wife and two children, while trying to maintain a public image that portrayed him as a devoted family man. Fisher was an avid hunter and outdoor enthusiast—neighbors and friends noted that he had shot a stray dog, fired shots into the air to scare a picnicking family, and once smeared the blood of an elk he shot on his face. Neighbors also stated that it was common to hear Mary and Robert yelling, and most friends knew their marriage was unhappy. In 2000, Fisher confided in a coworker that he had contracted a UTI from a prostitute and worried that Mary would leave him.

On April 9, 2001, at around 10:00 p.m., a neighbor heard a loud argument from inside the Fishers' home, and investigators believe this is around the time Fisher murdered his wife and two children. At 10:43 p.m., Fisher was spotted on an ATM camera, where he withdrew $280 and was seen driving Mary's car. At 4:42 a.m. on April 10, the house exploded and subsequently had several smaller explosions caused by ammunition or paint cans; firefighters were able to determine that Fisher most likely set up the explosion after killing his family. Police have theorized that Fisher murdered his family because he did not want his children to suffer as he had because of his parents' divorce.

On April 20, police found Mary's car in Tonto National Forest, 100 miles north of Scottsdale, Arizona, where the murders occurred. The family dog was found outside the car, as well as a hat identical to the one Fisher was wearing in the ATM footage. Police searched the area but found no sign of Fisher, but many professional cavers believe that Fisher hid in the complex underground network of caves and either escaped, committed suicide, or died from low oxygen. A couple believed they saw Fisher on April 10 in the Fort Apache Indian Reservation. Although there have been alleged sightings in Canada, Arizona, and Colorado, investigators have not been able to find any evidence of Fisher's whereabouts.

SUSAN WALSH

Susan Walsh, born Susan Young in 1960, was an American writer and free-lance journalist who went missing in 1996. At the time of her disappearance, she lived in an apartment complex with her son, David, and her estranged husband, Mark, who lived in the apartment below them. Walsh was also enrolled in a master's program in English at New York University, which she was halfway through completing, supporting her son by working as a freelance journalist and occasional stripper.

On July 16, 1996, Walsh left her apartment to run errands and make a phone call at the telephone booth across the street, leaving her son in the care of Mark. Susan was never seen again.

Police were quickly able to eliminate Mark as a suspect, and many of her friends believed that she may have relapsed after eleven years of drug sobriety.

While there were very few clues for investigators to follow, several rumors circulated about Walsh's disappearance being connected to some of the investigative journalism she had been conducting. Walsh wrote an in-depth investigation in *The Village Voice* about members of the Russian Mafia who were allegedly forcing young girls into the sex industry through a strip club ring. Shortly after that article was published, Walsh wrote an unpublished article about an underground vampire community in New York City; however, police found no evidence linking Walsh's disappearance to either the Russian Mafia or the vampire community.

Two days before her disappearance, Walsh was interviewed for a documentary, *Stripped,* where she stated that she had a stalker. She also contributed research, photographs, and personal writings to the book *Red Light: Inside the Sex Industry.* A former boyfriend of Walsh's came forward in 2006, stating that another ex of hers had been following her in the days leading up to her disappearance; Mark refused to let police do forensic testing inside their home. Despite this, no one has been charged with any crimes related to Walsh's disappearance and her whereabouts remain a mystery.

ERIN MARIE GILBERT

Erin Marie Gilbert was an American woman who disappeared in 1995 while attending the Girdwood Forest Fair in Girdwood, Alaska. Originally from San Francisco, California, Gilbert moved to Alaska, where she moved in with her sister, Stephanie, and Stephanie's husband at the Elmendorf Air Force Base. Gilbert took a job as a nanny for a family that was acquainted with Stephanie, and had plans to go to beauty school.

On July 1, 1995, Gilbert was picked up by David Combs, a man she met at a bar in Anchorage, and they went to the Girdwood Forest Fair in a small village south of Anchorage. Gilbert was last seen at the fair's beer garden with Combs, before leaving with him at around 6:00 p.m. According to Combs, he and Gilbert returned to the car, but the battery was dead because he left the headlights on. Combs left Gilbert to go in search of a nearby friend's house for assistance but was unable to find it. After searching for the house for around two hours, Combs returned to the car, but Gilbert was missing. Combs assumed she had taken off and returned to the fair, where he searched for her until around 1:00 a.m.

Combs called Gilbert's sister at 7:00 a.m. that morning to make sure that she had gotten home all right. Stephanie and her family searched the Girdwood Forest and its surrounding woods the morning of July 2. Alaska State Troopers organized an aerial and dog search for Gilbert but were unable to locate any sign of her. Gilbert's family has offered a $35,000 reward for any information about her disappearance. There have been no leads in the case. Gilbert is one of around 1,520 missing people in Alaska.

JENNIFER KESSE

Jennifer Kesse was an American woman who disappeared in 2006. At the time of her disappearance, Kesse was living in Orlando, Florida, and was working at the Central Florida Investments Timeshare Company as a finance manager.

On January 22, 2006, she and her boyfriend returned from a vacation in Saint Croix, US Virgin Islands. She stayed at her boyfriend's home that night. On Monday, January 23, Kesse left her boyfriend's house to go to her job in Ocoee. Kesse was last seen leaving work at around 6:00 p.m. At 6:15 p.m., she spoke to her father on the phone, and at around 10:00 p.m., she spoke to her boyfriend. Kesse did not arrive at work the next morning and her boyfriend's call went directly to voicemail. Her employer contacted her parents, who traveled from Tampa and found nothing strange about her apartment but noted her car was missing. Her parents found a wet towel and other items that led them to believe she had gotten ready for work that morning.

On the evening of January 24, family, friends, and the Orlando Police Department organized a search party and distributed flyers. Two days later, authorities found Kesse's car and security footage that showed a person parking Kesse's car approximately 1.2 miles away from her home at 12:00 p.m. on January 24 and subsequently walking away. The footage did not show any discernible features, and a neighboring fence blocked any good view of the person of interest. Kesse's car was searched for evidence, and only a small DNA fiber and a latent print were found.

Investigators believe that robbery was not a motive, and the suspect wiped down the car. Kesse's cell phone, iPod, keys, purse, briefcase, and outfit were all missing. Kesse's apartment complex was under construction at the time, and she had told family members that the workers often catcalled and harassed her, but none were found to be suspicious. Kesse's computer revealed that a manager at her job had tried to initiate a relationship with her but she had turned him down; he was also eliminated as a suspect. In 2010, the FBI took over the case, and there have been no further leads.

In 2008, the Florida House of Representatives passed "The Jennifer Kesse and Tiffany Sessions Missing Persons Act" to change how missing persons cases are investigated in Florida.

ROBERT LEVINSON

Robert Levinson was an American federal agent who went missing in 2007 in Kish Island, Iran, and is believed to have been held captive by the government of Iran.

Levinson worked for several government agencies, including the Drug Enforcement Administration (1970–1976), the Federal Bureau of Investigation (1976–1998), and the Central Intelligence Agency (1998–2007), the latter of which he was on a mission for at the time of his disappearance.

While the US government initially denied that Levinson was working for the government when he went missing, the Associated Press reported in 2013 that he had been working for the CIA. It was revealed that Levinson had been on an unauthorized intelligence-gathering mission, and the trip was planned by three CIA officials who had not gotten proper approval for the mission. Kish Island is a free-trade zone, meaning that Levinson did not need a visa to enter the country and was set to meet his source, Dawud Salahuddin, a fugitive who was accused of killing an Iranian diplomat, Ali Akbar Tabatabaei, in 1980.

Levinson's wife, Christine, and his eldest son, Dan, traveled to Iran against the wishes of the United States Department of State to investigate his disappearance. Christine and Dan met with Iranian officials and were able to see Levinson's hotel, his signature on his checkout bill, and flight manifests from planes that left Kish when Levinson was scheduled to leave the country. The officials promised to give the family a full investigative report but have not done so as of 2022.

Although the Iranian government denied any involvement in Levinson's disappearance, Levinson's family released a hostage video of Levinson in 2010 and photos of him wearing an orange jumpsuit with overgrown hair in 2013. US officials believe that Iran's intelligence service is behind the 2010 hostage video, due to its tradecraft. Both President George W. Bush and President Barack Obama, in 2007 and 2013, respectively, released statements on Levinson's case, ensured the public that it was still a high priority, and urged the Iranian government to release information about his whereabouts.

On May 11, 2015, the US Senate voted on a concurrent resolution for the release of three Americans arrested by Iran, as well as cooperation with the US government in locating and returning Levinson. In 2020, the US government declared Levinson legally dead and believed he had died in Iranian custody prior to 2020. A US court ordered the government of Iran to pay upward of $1.4 billion in punitive and compensatory damages to the Levinson family, which will be taken from the Iranian assets that were frozen in 1980 by the US government.

MATTEO "DIABOLIK" MESSINA DENARO

Matteo Messina Denaro, also known as "Diabolik" or "The Skinny," is a Sicilian Mafia boss who has been a fugitive on Italy's most wanted list since 1993, and is considered by *Forbes* to be one of the top ten most wanted criminals in the world.

Messina Denaro was born to the head of the Mafia Commission in Trapani, Sicily. Messina Denaro is reported to have learned how to shoot a gun at age fourteen and killed his first person at eighteen; he is believed to have killed at least fifty people. He became notorious for murdering rival Mafia boss Vincenzo Milazzo and his pregnant girlfriend. Messina Denaro began as an armed guard for the D'Alì family and soon became an overseer of their estate land holdings. After his father's death, Messina Denaro became the head of the area and some of the surrounding areas. Messina Denaro made his fortune from extorting businesses for protection money, skimming from construction contracts, the international drug trade, and a few legitimate businesses, including a supermarket chain, olive groves, and a corrupted oil production.

After being involved in several bombings that killed over twelve people and left ninety-three injured in 1992 and 1993, Messina Denaro went into hiding. Messina Denaro's lover, Maria Mesi, and her brother, Francesco, were arrested in 2000 and sentenced to three years in prison for aiding and abetting Messina Denaro. Messina Denaro was sentenced to life in prison in absentia in 2002 for his role in the bombings. In 2010, authorities seized many of Messina Denaro's assets, totaling over a billion euros. After the deaths of Bernardo Provenzano and Salvatore Riina, Messina Denaro is believed to be "the boss of all bosses" of the Italian Mafia.

Police believe that Messina Denaro is still in charge of the organization and is moving between safe houses near his family's home in Castelvetrano, but he still evades authorities.

ASSATA SHAKUR

Assata Olugbala Shakur, born JoAnne Deborah Byron, is an American political activist who is wanted by the FBI. A native New Yorker, Shakur was taken in by her aunt, Evelyn A. Williams, a civil rights worker living in Manhattan who helped her earn her GED. Shakur attended the Borough of Manhattan Community College and College of New York in the mid-1960s, where she became involved in civil rights protests, sit-ins, and political activities.

After graduating from college, Shakur moved to Oakland, California, and joined the Black Panther Party. She left the BPP and joined the Black Liberation Army, and they began a campaign of "guerilla activities" against the US government. In 1971, Shakur adopted her new name. Starting in 1971, Shakur was involved in several robberies and assault incidents in the New York area and was shot in the stomach after a struggle at the Statler Hilton Hotel. Between 1971 and 1973, in both New York and New Jersey, Shakur was charged with several crimes, including attempted robberies, assault, reckless endangerment, kidnapping, murder, attempted murder, and possession of a deadly weapon. These charges resulted in two mistrials, a hung jury, a change of venue, and three acquittals.

On May 2, 1973, Shakur was involved in a shootout on the New Jersey Turnpike, which was the only official charge she was convicted of, after a change of venue and mistrial, in 1977. Shakur was imprisoned in Rikers Island Correctional Institution for Women, where she was kept in solitary confinement for twenty-one months. Shakur gave birth to her only daughter in 1974 at the Elmhurst General Hospital, and she claimed in her autobiography that she had been beaten and restrained by officers after being denied a medical exam shortly after giving birth.

She was moved to several different prisons in New York and New Jersey, where she was subjected to poor treatment, including twenty-four-hour surveillance with no adequate medical attention, no exercise, no company from other women, and frequent vaginal and anal searches. Shakur was identified as a political prisoner by Angela Davis.

In 1979, a group of Black Liberation Army members called "The Family" began to plan Shakur's escape. On November 2, 1979, Shakur escaped from the Clinton Correctional Facility for Women in New Jersey with help from members of the BLA, and no prison officers were harmed. Shakur was believed to have lived in Pittsburgh for a time before fleeing to the Bahamas. For several years after her escape, the FBI circulated wanted posters for Shakur and continued to search for her. She was charged with unlawful flight to avoid imprisonment. By 1984, Shakur was granted political asylum in Cuba, and in 1985, her daughter came to live with her. Throughout the years, the US government has attempted to extradite Shakur, but none of the attempts have ever been successful. Shakur has also published a handful of autobiographies and books.

GEDHUN CHOEKYI NYIMA

Gedhun Choekyi Nyima is the eleventh Panchen Lama, a Tibetan Buddhist figure with high spiritual authority who is in charge of finding the next Dalai Lama. On May 14, 1995, Nyima was recognized publicly by the fourteenth Dalai Lama, Gyalwa Rinpoche. After the tenth Panchen Lama's death in 1989, the search for someone to be recognized as his reincarnation began under a cloud of mystery and controversy, as Tibet was under the control of the antireligious government of the People's Republic of China.

The head of the Panchen Lama search committee, Chadrel Rinpoche, worked with the Dalai Lama and Beijing authorities to find the next Panchen Lama. After naming six-year-old Gedhun Choekyi Nyima as the eleventh incarnation of the Panchen Lama, Chadrel Rinpoche was arrested and charged with treason. Chadrel Rinpoche was replaced by the Chinese Communist Party, who chose Gyancain Norbu as the next Panchen Lama, although he was rejected by most Tibetans. Three days after being named the Panchen Lama, Gedhun Choekyi Nyima was kidnapped by the Chinese government. Gedhun Choekyi Nyima and his family have remained forcibly detained by the Chinese government at an undisclosed location since his disappearance in 1995.

Chinese officials have maintained that Gedhun Choekyi Nyima's where-abouts are unknown to the public in order to protect him. Human rights organizations, including the United Nations Committee on the Rights of the Child, have requested to know the location of Gedhun Choekyi Nyima, to no avail, and he is believed by some to be a political prisoner. The Chinese government has maintained that Gedhun Choekyi Nyima and his family are safe and leading a normal life. In 2007, China failed to respond to Asma Jahangir, Special Rapporteur on Freedom of Religion or Belief on the UN Human Rights Council, when she asked what measures had been taken to ensure his safety, and requested an independent expert to confirm Gedhun Choekyi Nyima's well-being.

In 2018, the Dalai Lama stated that he knew from a reliable source that Gedhun Choekyi Nyima was safe and receiving a normal education. According to the Chinese government, Gedhun Choekyi Nyima is alive and well and attending university; however, he has not been seen by an independent source since 1995.

THE SPRINGFIELD THREE: SHERRILL LEVITT, SUZANNE "SUZIE" STREETER, AND STACY MCCALL

Single mother Sherrill Levitt, her nineteen-year-old daughter, Suzie Streeter, and Suzie's eighteen-year-old friend Stacy McCall were last seen on June 7, 1992. The previous day, McCall and Streeter graduated from Kickapoo High School in Springfield, Missouri, and had been attending graduation parties in Springfield and nearby Battlefield. The two girls planned to spend the night at their friend Janelle Kirby's house but decided to go to Streeter's home, where she lived with her mother, Sherrill. Investigators believe they arrived at the house, because their clothing, purses, and cars were all at the Levitt/Streeter house. Levitt was last heard from on June 6 around 11:00 p.m., when she spoke on the phone with a friend.

On June 7, Kirby and her boyfriend went to the house. Neither Streeter nor McCall had returned to Kirby's home, where they were supposed to meet to go to a water park. While all three of the women's cars were parked outside, Kirby and her boyfriend found no sign of any of the women. Kirby reported to police that she saw that the shade of the porch lamp was shattered, and her boyfriend swept it up. Inside the house, Kirby found Levitt and Streeter's dog, Cinnamon, who appeared agitated. Kirby also picked up two phone calls to the home phone, where an unidentified male made strange sexual innuendos. A few hours later, McCall's mother, Janis, visited the house after failing to hear from her daughter and called the police when she found all three women's purses on the floor of the living room. Janis McCall also listened to a strange message on the answering machine, but it was erased from the tape by the time police arrived.

Police were unable to find any physical evidence, due to the high volume of concerned friends and family that came to the home in search of the women, and the fact that the women had been missing for more than sixteen hours before it was reported. Despite thousands of tips from the

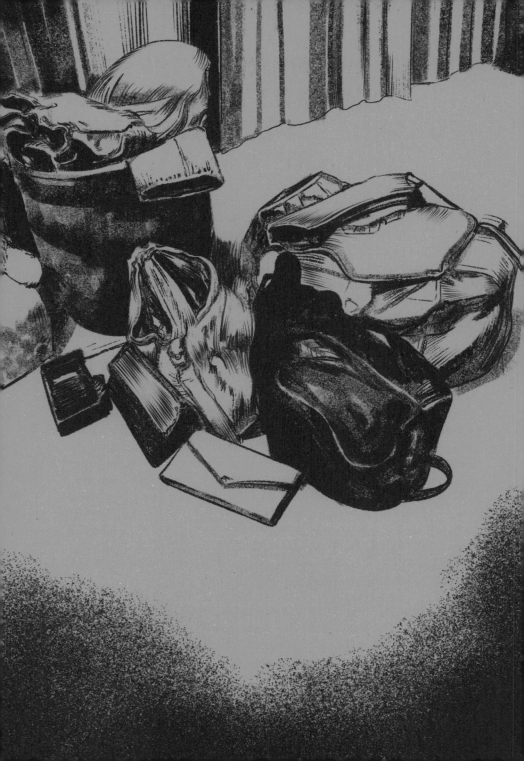

public, police were unable to find any conclusive evidence about the missing women, besides witnesses claiming to see a green van near the home.

In 2003, a tip was called in to search farmland near Cassville, where they found possible blood and a section of a green vehicle, but the blood evidence was inconclusive. Robert Craig Cox, who was in prison for a murder in Florida, claimed to know information about the women and stated that he knew they were dead, but he had an alibi, and investigators found no further evidence that Cox was involved in their disappearance. McCall and Streeter were declared legally dead in 1997, but all three women are still filed as missing persons.

Now that you know the facts of the most mysterious disappearances on record, you'll have to decide for yourself how these stories ended. Can you explain the unexplained? Have you noticed some small clue that has eluded investigators for years? It's possible that your eyes are the first to focus on what others have missed. Or are these mysteries meant to remain exactly that—mysteries? Whether you believe that there are supernatural reasons for these instances or that there is undiscovered evidence hiding right under our noses, you've become part of the great human tradition of seeking the answers that elude us. Here's to hoping that those who were lost are one day found.